© 2020 Connor Boyack

All rights reserved.

No graphic, visual, electronic, film, microfilm, tape recording, or any other means may be used to reproduce in any form, without prior written permission of the author, except in the case of brief passages embodied in critical reviews and articles.

ISBN 978-1-943521-53-1

Boyack, Connor, author.
Stanfield, Elijah, illustrator.
Weber, Brenden, editor.
The Tuttle Twins Guide to Inspiring Entrepreneurs / Connor Boyack.

Cover design by Elijah Stanfield
Edited and typeset by Connor Boyack

Printed in the United States

10 9 8 7 6 5 4 3 2 1

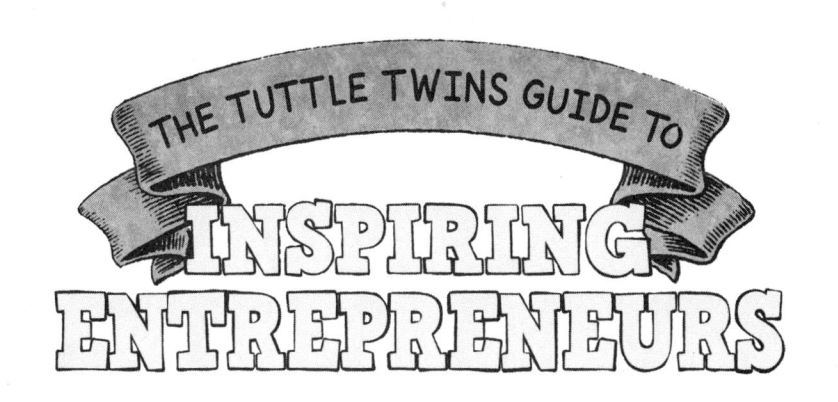

THE TUTTLE TWINS GUIDE TO INSPIRING ENTREPRENEURS

BY CONNOR BOYACK

The List of ENTREPRENEURS

Adi Dassler 1

Brian Chesky & Joe Gebbia 11

Andrew Mellon 23

Elijah McCoy 37

Elon Musk 47

George Eastman 59

Hetty Green 71

Howard Schultz 79

John Rockefeller 91

Madam Walker 101

Magatte Wade 109

Powel Crosley 119

Steve Jobs 131

Wally Amos 141

Walt Disney 151

Yvon Chouinard 163

If you're anything like us, you want to figure out how to be successful in life. And what we've learned over the years is that learning how to become an entrepreneur is a ticket to success.

Many of you have followed our adventures when we were younger, as we learned about business, marketing, risk, money, and more. All of this information is *so* essential if we want to succeed!

But over the years we have been able to learn from the lives of people who have been down this path before us—whose hard work and experiences give us some insight into what life as an entrepreneur might look like.

So we did some research for you on a bunch of amazing people who have a lot to teach us—and you!—about what it takes to succeed. As you read their stories, pay close attention to the lessons you can learn and apply in your own life.

It's also important to realize that part of success is learning from failure. Many of these people ran into big problems that they had to tackle. The sign of a true entrepreneur is not giving up—realizing that trying again and again gives you the experience and wisdom to eventually succeed!

Many kids our age throw their hands up in frustration when they face a setback. But we know it's important to see these obstacles as challenges that will strengthen us and help us more in the future.

Another thing we've learned is that entrepreneurship is about service—when you help solve other people's problems, they'll reward you! Creating products and services that improve others' lives helps them, and in exchange, helps us as well! It's a real win-win.

So we hope you enjoy this material we put together for you and expect you to learn just as much as we have! Together, let's figure out how to become amazing entrepreneurs and help make the world a better place!

—The Tuttle Twins

People may call me the father of the modern sports industry, but all I am is an athlete that saw a benefit to improving equipment.

Adi
DASSLER

Driven to achieve greater athletic performance, Adolf Dassler overcame wars, dictators, poverty, and social norms to change the world of sports forever.

"A bad idea is always better than none at all. Only by trying can the wrong become right."

More than a Pair of Shoes

Imagine walking down a busy street in the largest city you have ever visited. Now, look down at the feet of the people walking past you. As you are taking your imaginary stroll down the street staring at feet, you notice three stripes on some pairs of shoes. Which brand comes immediately to mind? Adidas.

Behind every great brand, product, or invention is a creator who dared to try something new. An entrepreneur who saw a problem facing society or their area of interest and took a step back to allow their creative energy to imagine a new solution. The creator of Adidas was just a man looking to solve a problem for the hobby he loved. He was a sports fanatic looking to improve the performance of those who loved to compete in the games he loved. His name is Adolf Dassler.

Competitive Spirit

Dassler, called Adi by those who knew him, was born on November 3, 1900, as the fourth child of Christoph and Pauline Dassler. His older brother Rudolf was born two years before, and these two brothers encouraged each other through friendly competition.

During their childhood, Adi and Rudolf found sports to be a way to express their competitive spirits. Nobody likes to lose, even during friendly competition amongst siblings. But, losing to his older brother helped fuel Adi's motivation. It made him stop and think, "What can I do to enhance my performance?" Questions like these would stick in his mind into his adult life.

In 1913, after finishing up his education, Dassler's father wanted him to begin an apprenticeship to become a baker. Although he worked to fulfill his father's wishes, after his working hours were over, his mind shifted back to his true passion—sports. As time passed, so did his desire to find a way to make money by doing the thing he loved.

He had to find a way to live off of his passion. Dassler just so happened to grow up in the small town of Herzogenaurach, Germany, with a population of only around 4,000 people. This small town was unique. It had a large number of shoemakers in its very small community. In 1922 the town had 112 shoemakers; it was the shoemaking hub of Germany.

Dassler found himself interested in the process of shoemaking as he began to realize the importance of the shoes on his feet. He turned to his father, who worked at one of the shoe factories. From him, Dassler was able to gather some knowledge of the process. But, living among so many shoemakers, Dassler knew that the market was already full of talented people who made high-quality products. Where was the gap in the market?

Dassler needed to find a unique problem to solve within the shoemaking market he found so fascinating.

Finding the Problem

Dassler was fascinated with a broad spectrum of sports including track and field, soccer, hockey, boxing, and more. His experience with a broad spectrum of sports allowed him to develop a thorough understanding of the various types of equipment that was needed for different sports.

For example, for track and field, you have a starting point in the race and an endpoint. For hockey, you use a puck, hockey stick, and ice skates. For soccer, you need a designated goal area and a ball to score in the goal.

Dassler was able to step back and consider what every athlete needed for top performance: a comfortable, durable, and reliable pair of shoes. During his time, this was something that was hard to come by.

With Dassler filling all of his free time playing any sports activity he could find, it was no surprise he found baking uninspiring. However, he had made a promise to his father, and he understood the importance of following through with his promises. He fulfilled his apprenticeship, but upon completion, he was ready to take on his passion-driven interest: tackling the obstacles facing the sporting world.

Dassler had recognized another issue besides the lack of high-quality footwear: the lack of specialized footwear for each individual sport. Consider the options free enterprise has brought us today. You have shoes specially made for almost every sport: football, basketball, soccer, hockey, etc. These specialized shoes have been optimized to meet the needs of each sport, but they have not existed as long as the sports have. Someone like Dassler had to take the time to consider the needs of each sport and design a shoe to address those needs. Before sports innovators such as Dassler, everyone wore the same type of shoes for all sports. The market was looking for someone to step up!

Dassler became convinced that specialized shoes for various sports would improve performance. Someone just needed to act.

Road Block

As Dassler began to think seriously about his problem, he faced a major roadblock: World War I.

War is destructive. It brings death, carnage, and an end to the innovative progression of society. For someone like Dassler, who was drafted in 1918 by Germany, there was no way to pursue his creative dreams while the fighting continued. Instead, he was forcefully compelled to fulfill an authoritarian obligation to the government.

The destructive nature of war was not over after the guns stopped firing though. The catastrophic effects of WWI on Germany included both economic and emotional depressions. People were not interested in buying products because they were not in a financial position to do so. For many, the war had brought heartbreak, sadness, economic strife, and a grim outlook on life. This was no environment for Dassler's creative vision to bloom.

Dassler was still determined to pursue his plan after the war, but he faced another obstacle: a severe lack of resources.

He had to get creative. To produce the shoes, Dassler used an old milling machine he rigged up himself. Electricity was scarce after the war, so he found himself improvising by placing an old bicycle within the milling machine on wooden beams to enable the device to be pedal-powered. He then used old war materials to produce the shoes, focusing on durable, lightweight materials that would create an airy shoe that was more supportive for athletic activity.

Dassler sent samples of his shoes to sports clubs around

the region. He took the opportunity to demonstrate their quality. In return, players, managers, and trainers from around the area stood in line to place their orders.

Brothers on the Forefront of Innovation

Adi Dassler was the focused inventor while Rudolf was the more extroverted salesman. This combination worked out for Dassler, as it allowed him to focus on his craft and remain ahead of the market. Combined, they founded the Dassler Brothers' Sports Shoe Factory.

The two brothers are known for creating the first soccer shoes made with leather studs and track shoes made with metal spikes. Adi continually worked to make all of the shoes more lightweight and durable. This made them the best athletic shoe on the market for almost any sport.

Dassler was highly confident about his creations. He put time, effort, and thought into his products to ensure they met his standards of perfection. Finally, after working to refine his designs, he was ready to show them off to the world.

The Summer Olympics in 1928 were a turning point for the young shoe company. At the time, athletes didn't pay much attention to the equipment they used; they thought their talent could carry them all the way. Dassler saw things differently. He wanted athletes to use his shoes to enhance their performance. He provided the German distance runner Lina Radke with a pair of track shoes specially developed for track and field distance runners. The shoes were equipped with six lightweight spikes to provide more grip. This was unheard of at the time. Wearing Dassler's creation, Radke went on to break the world record for the 800 meters and won a gold medal.

On the world stage, Dassler proved that athletes could run faster, run farther, jump higher, and be more agile with specialized shoes. Everyone saw the innovative power of Dassler's visionary creation, forever cementing his place in the history of sports.

Conclusion

The two brothers continued creating innovative athletic wear; however, their business relationship became strained after World War II. Adi was focused on continuing to develop and innovate their footwear, while Rudolf wanted to expedite the shoemaking process. Dassler wanted quality over quantity; Rudolf was focused on quantity over quality.

Their disagreements were insurmountable, and the two split in 1948. This was the moment when Adidas was born. But that's not all. An infamous rivalry began as Rudolf launched the successful company Puma. Both companies continue to pioneer lightweight footwear into the present.

After Dassler's death in 1978, the family-owned company continued focusing on developing innovative products to remain on top of the athletic equipment market. They added sporting clothes, soccer balls, tennis balls, rackets, and many other sporting product lines. As of today, Adidas competes with Nike for the number one spot in the global market for sports gear.

But for Dassler, playing sports was a platform for building unity. It was a place where athletes could compete without focusing on their political affiliation, religious faith, or ethnicity. The focus was on the competition at hand: who was the best athlete playing the game of the moment. It was a way for people to forget about the problems facing the world, a place for everyone to decompress from life's stresses.

Fun Facts

- Adidas is the second largest manufacturer of sportswear in the world and the largest in Europe.

- Dassler equipped African-American track star Jesse Owens with track shoes; Owens then went on to win four gold medals.

Airbnb was born out of necessity. Our rent went up. It was born out of a problem.
...but it wasn't meant to be the company we were trying to start.
airbnb

Brian CHESKY
Joe GEBBIA

Two college roommates struggling to pay their own rent hatched a plan to rent out space to people traveling from out of town. Ultimately, this idea provided a way for others to make extra money using their empty home space, disrupting a multi-billion dollar industry.

"We've invented a new marketplace. There was no easy way to rent a person's bedroom over the Internet or book a vacation rental over the Internet. There was no guidebook for us to turn to as we defined this new marketplace."

We've Never Met, but I'm Here to Stay

Rapid technological advancements have altered today's society more than anyone could have ever anticipated. With the power of the Internet in the hands of many individuals, the world has experienced numerous changes to markets that nobody predicted.

The technological boom experienced within society has strongly impacted educational fields, areas of research, and personal entertainment. However, these are not the only changes. One of the most influential fields today is innovation and entrepreneurship. It plays an influential role in almost every area of our lives, whether we realize it or not!

In the past, it was difficult to start one's own business to bring a new idea to life, but with the modern advancements in technology, this is no longer the case. While the financial aspects of starting a business can still be a hurdle, the process has become much simpler. For example, some companies now solely market products through the Internet—think of Amazon or Netflix—while others use the Internet as an advertising platform to sell or rent products for their physical business, such as Lowe's and Best Buy.

That's the power of the free market shining through!

Furthermore, the Internet has allowed companies to advertise more easily. Because the Internet is so easily accessed by most individuals, this technological world has provided the power to attempt a business venture from the comfort of one's home, office, or apartment.

The story of Brian Chesky and Joe Gebbia, the founders of

Airbnb, shows that while starting a business out of one's apartment might be difficult, the Internet has made it possible for individuals with a timely idea to go from worrying about paying rent to building a business worth over a billion dollars.

This is the entrepreneurial story of how Brian Chesky and Joe Gebbia made sleeping in a stranger's home normal.

A Dynamic Duo

Brian Chesky and Joe Gebbia did not come from money, but they had supportive homes. One might be curious how they gained the renown and success that they possess today. Neither had entrepreneurially-minded parents to teach them the ways of the free market, although both sets of parents were supportive of their child's endeavors. Sometimes that's all a child needs.

Chesky and Gebbia were simply open to opportunities and willing to follow their passion.

In the case of Gebbia, he always held a passion for drawing. As a kid he loved the Teenage Mutant Ninja Turtles. He spent hours drawing his favorite characters, and his classmates started to notice. They wanted a drawing of their own!

Gebbia had the inclinations of an entrepreneur from the start. So, when his classmates started asking for his drawings, he started charging $1 to $2, depending on the size. Demand kept rising, and profits were coming in; business was booming.

But the grade school kids were using their lunch money to pay for the drawings. Unfortunately for Gebbia, the parents caught on, and a teacher shut down his operation.

This became a lesson for him. As he put it, "You could say it was my first brush with regulation." It wouldn't be his last.

Chesky and Gebbia met during their college experience at the Rhode Island School of Design (RISD). Despite their shared backgrounds and experiences, it would not be until after they graduated that they would begin to work together.

After graduating from RISD, Chesky moved across the country to Los Angeles where he began to work. Shortly after, Gebbia moved to San Francisco. In 2007, Gebbia finally convinced Chesky to move to San Francisco, where they became roommates. That's when Gebbia came up with the idea that would become a billion-dollar company.

Staying with Strangers?

In 2007, a local conference took place in San Francisco, and every room in the local hotels was booked. At the time, Chesky and Gebbia were struggling to make ends meet and were attempting to develop different ways to make money so that they would be able to pay their rent by the end of the month.

Inspired by all the booked rooms, Gebbia emailed Chesky with an idea. Gebbia told Chesky that he had come up with a way to make money by turning their residence into a "Designer's bed-and-breakfast." The living space would provide individuals a place to stay for four days during the local event.

"We built a basic website, and Air Bed and Breakfast was born," Gebbia said. "Three lucky guests got to stay on a $20 airbed on the hardwood floor. But they loved it. And so did we."

An idea that started off as a way to make some extra cash over a long weekend turned into a pivotal business idea.

During this time, the pair took to developing what was then known as Airbedandbreakfast.com. Their new website allowed their guests to book the rooms in their home.

This concept was only the beginning of what eventually became Airbnb. It took much more effort to develop the idea into the company it is today.

In 2008, things began to make a turn for Chesky and Gebbia. During this year, Chesky and Gebbia had become concerned because their combined debt was reaching over $30,000, and despite their business being roughly a year and a half old, the website was only producing 10 to 20 bookings daily.

It was at this time that Chesky and Gebbia decided to stand out from the rest by focusing on the "breakfast" over the "bed" in their bed and breakfast business plan. During the presidential campaign, Chesky and Gebbia created 1,000 collectible boxes of cereal titled Obama O's and Cap'n McCain's which individuals could purchase for $40 a box. To their surprise, this move generated enough profit to pull them out of their debt. It helped keep their company afloat until it became part of a start-up accelerator known as Y Combinator based out of Silicon Valley in 2009.

During their time at Y Combinator, they received advice from the Y Combinator co-founder, Paul Graham. Graham explained to Chesky that while their company still had a small number of customers, they should take the time to approach each user and customer and get to know them. While it seemed slightly unrealistic to Chesky at the time, Chesky began to travel from California to New York where he and Gebbia would meet with each of their clients while pretending to be photographers.

"The first thing [Graham] told us was 'It's better to have 100 people that love you more than a million people that just sort of like you," Chesky once said. "Find 100 people that love you... I think that's the challenge that most people have when they try to start a business—but almost all great movements in history, all great products start with a core base of people. And the good news is that you can do things that don't scale. So you can start with a few people and do things that large companies can't do."

During one of these ventures to New York, Chesky asked one of the customers if he had any feedback. The man gave Chesky a binder that included a plethora of notes and feedback. This notebook provided Chesky and Gebbia with details, tips, and advice that would serve as a roadmap for the development of Airbnb. Such a simple idea was crucial for expanding their idea—simply getting information from the customers they were providing for!

Airbnb is still privately owned, and during 2017, the company was worth $31 billion. However, the founders did not get their company to this point without hard work and dedication. There are many lessons to take from their experiences.

Chesky and Gebbia both give a lot of credit to their college experience and education. Not only did their college experience allow their paths to cross, but the classes and lessons learned during that time helped sculpt them into the people they are today. During interviews, Gebbia states that art school is what helped him be an entrepreneur, and Chesky's childhood potential for leadership became more pronounced during his time at RISD.

Ultimately, there are at least three critical lessons you should take away from this story.

Lessons from the Journey

The first lesson from the adventures of Chesky and Gebbia: one should not be afraid to take a chance. Chesky and Gebbia were in a bind when they were attempting to pay the rent; however, taking a chance on a good idea helped carry them from unemployed college graduates to a net worth of a billion dollars. During the start-up of their business, there were times Chesky and Gebbia were worried about their future. Chesky has stated that during their first year, only 50 people a day were visiting their website. As they attempted to start the business and cover all other expenses, they had gone into debt.

Chesky and Gebbia took a series of chances on ideas as they tried to pay the rent. First, in renting out space in their own apartment, and again as they developed the idea for collectible cereal boxes which carried them out of their $30,000 debt and into a new phase for their business. Had Chesky or Gebbia hesitated or refused to take a chance on their ideas out of fear, they might not be the multibillionaires they are today.

They had a passion and never lost sight of it. It was something they believed in, and they were literally ready to go broke for it.

A second lesson from Chesky and Gebbia is that an individual, whether starting a business or not, should never ignore the advice of others. Airbnb was built by Chesky and Gebbia because they were willing to listen to suggestions offered by others. When Chesky or Gebbia were presented with advice, they made it a point to listen, consider, and often implement the advice. They accepted their own ignorance!

This includes advice regarding their personal lives. As previously mentioned, Gebbia credits his college experience for making him the person he is today; however, the reason Gebbia eventually attended RISD was due to a suggestion given to him by a teacher at the Atlanta College of Art. Furthermore, without the suggestions presented to Chesky and Gebbia by the co-founder of Y Combinator or the suggestion notebook given to them by a customer, Airbnb might not have ever come to be what it is now.

Both of them were willing to listen and learn.

A lot of the success Chesky and Gebbia have is due to their understanding that others have a lot to offer. Taking the advice presented to them helped steer Chesky and Gebbia in the direction they needed to take to become successful.

A final lesson to be learned from these two young billionaires is that one should never give up on a dream because of a rough patch. There were countless times before, during, and after Airbnb's start-up where the business and its founders struggled. As previously mentioned, after graduation, the two creators had very little money. They then acquired $30,000 of debt. Later, they experienced an issue regarding a large company flaw they never anticipated; a property whose owner was a customer of Airbnb was robbed. Eventually, this issue was fixed by Chesky issuing a formal apology and promising individuals that they were covered for $50,000 when using Airbnb. But, these are not the only struggles they have faced.

Today Airbnb is still struggling with different state laws, city ordinances, policies, and much more. The laws are often instituted to protect the hotel industry, which is worried about Airbnb's market innovation hurting their bottom line. But the duo believes in the service they provide: connecting travelers with a customized, homey, short-term rental option.

They have given property owners an avenue to share their beautiful homes with their fellow humans.

In the face of constant government attacks, Chesky and Gebbia continue to work on new ways to help their business overcome these struggles and continue. While many of these government-enforced obstacles could have stopped the progress of Airbnb, Chesky and Gebbia were determined not to let bumps in the road bring their dream to a halt. Thus, one of the most important lessons one should take away from these Airbnb founders is that with persistence and determination, one can turn a rough patch into a multibillion-dollar company.

In the end, society has embraced the idea of staying in strangers' homes.

With the development of the Internet and a technological boom, individuals have more opportunities to test their entrepreneurial skills and create a business. Brian Chesky and Joe Gebbia are two individuals who saw an opportunity and never looked back.

Using the Internet and tactful marketing, Chesky and Gebbia have developed a company that has provided them with money and opportunities they never imagined. While some say it's not possible, Airbnb's success proves that taking a chance, accepting the advice of others, and cultivating determination can turn someone from counting coins to being on the cover of Forbes Magazine.

Fun Facts

- Airbnb continues its fight against local ordinance and short-term rental laws today.

- As of 2020, there are around three million active Airbnb offers in 191 countries.

The spirit of business adventure is what has made this country the most prosperous in history.

Andrew MELLON

Though a very successful businessman, the greatest contribution Mellon made was not the wealth he created or gave away, but rather his policies while in government that allowed millions of other Americans to produce wealth.

"If the spirit of business adventure is killed, this country will cease to hold the foremost position in the world."

A Freedom Loving Politician

Throughout history, we have seen a trend where successful entrepreneurs, business owners, and CEOs remain in the world of business for their entire lives, continuing to innovate and expand. They leave politics to others, opting to stay in the field of industry to keep building upon their vision for a better world.

However, Andrew Mellon thought differently. Even as the third wealthiest American of his era, he felt compelled to enter the hostile world of politics, leaving behind his flourishing business career for political duty. Why the urge to enter the political arena? He saw the need for a business mindset in government, a voice to remind legislators of the problematic effects of over-regulating and overtaxing the people. He wanted to remind politicians how the real world works.

Mellon left the business world to become the secretary of the treasury for presidents Warren Harding, Calvin Coolidge, and Herbert Hoover. Although Mellon was among the most significant business minds of his era, his legacy is primarily remembered for the entrepreneurial mindset he brought to politics. He has a legacy as someone who mastered the world of business and the world of philanthropy, and then took those skills to master the world of politics. He implemented fiscal policies that allowed millions of individuals to flourish.

A Father Figure

In 1818, Andrew Mellon's father, Thomas Mellon, came to the United States from Ireland to live with his extended family. He was only 5 years old at the time. Like many others throughout the 1800s, Mellon's family chose to flee from the hardships facing those across the ocean: crop failure, overwhelming tax increases, and job shortages. Many looked to the United States for a fresh start and economic opportunity: a new place to call home with hopes of a better life.

Although Thomas Mellon first settled in Westmoreland County, Pennsylvania, he soon discovered farm life was not for him. When facing a crossroads between staying on the family farm or pursuing further ambitions, Thomas turned to books.

Thomas Mellon picked up a copy of Benjamin Franklin's autobiography and found himself captivated by each page. He read the book from cover to cover again and again to identify every golden nugget of information he could consume. This one book played the role of mentor for him, teaching him the principles to make his dreams and ambitions a reality. It solidified three principles: keep your goals in mind when taking action, keep your word to others, and use time efficiently by always being involved in something useful. Thomas Mellon used these three principles to formulate an entrepreneurial mindset that he would pass on to his children.

The Model Son

Andrew Mellon was the sixth child in the Mellon family. When his father's eyesight began to fail, Andrew helped him in his work as a judge by reading for him. This created a close bond between Andrew and his father. While Thomas acted as an advisor to his other sons, Andrew became more of a partner and apprentice. With the responsibility of being the designated reader for his father, Andrew gathered lessons from Darwin to Adam Smith on the principles of free markets that would help him develop his entrepreneurial state of mind. But Andrew had a resource beyond books; he had a mentor to help guide him on his journey into understanding the world of entrepreneurship.

Instead of pursuing traditional education from an institution, Andrew Mellon found himself working under an ideal teacher ready to share lessons learned from first-hand experience from the perspective of a successful business owner. With a more quiet and reserved character, he happened to be the perfect student to work under his father's assertive personality. His understanding of the need to absorb, listen and internally reflect on the principles he learned from his father made for an optimal mentor and apprentice partnership. His foundation for consuming the words of others helped him develop an innovative mindset for business.

Thomas Mellon eventually handed down their family bank, T. Mellon & Sons, to Andrew when he was merely 27 years old. Upon taking over the family business, many saw Andrew as having more of a laid back and cautious business mindset than the assertive, commanding attitude of his father. But Andrew understood the importance of consuming information from the lessons from his father, books, and those around him who had many more years in the business world. He learned to gather all possible information, analyze that information, and only then make a decision.

This reserved approach became part of his decision-making process. Andrew understood that to make the best decisions you have to focus on the *process* of decision making, not the outcome. Knowing that once he gathered and analyzed all of the right information, only then could he trust the outcome of his decision. This understanding led him to become one of the most successful business minds of his era.

Mellon as a Businessman

Many expected Andrew would continue the bank's operations in a modest but sustainable model. But they all missed Andrew's true intentions; he had great plans for expansion.

Mellon understood that to accomplish what he wanted in business, the money must become secondary. He learned from his father that you must create value first, but once you do that, money will inevitably follow.

For example, Mellon used his investment knowledge when Captain Alfred Ephraim Hunt, Arthur Vining Davis and George Clapp came to the Mellon bank seeking $4,000 in investment. They were selling a new up-and-coming product: industrial aluminum. The company presenting the idea was small. The technology was still relatively unproven. The team had yet to test the idea, but Andrew was ready to listen. He allowed the small company to present him with all the information on why this product would be successful, why it was the product of the future, and why he should invest.

Ultimately, Andrew offered them $25,000 instead of the $4,000 they'd requested. He was sold. He allowed himself to consider new information and the unproven technology. He knew he could live with the outcome. In the end, aluminum did become the product of the future for being durable and lightweight. It became the go-to product in numerous industries like construction, packaging, electricity, and transportation. And it's still widely used today.

Andrew would end up creating one of the largest financial empires in the world from steel, oil, shipbuilding, coal, banking, and aluminum. The lessons from his upbringing provided him with an impressive ability to pick technologies, businesses, and entrepreneurs who had a product of the future. His future-focused mindset, along with his reserved personality, helped prevent him from making impulsive decisions. Before making a significant business decision, Mellon would gather all the information his team could find so they could analyze their risks before moving forward. But once a decision was made, he was all in.

The Mellon Mindset in the Treasury

When he entered the world of politics, Andrew Mellon was the third wealthiest American of his era, behind only Henry Ford and John D. Rockefeller. However, his successful business contributions pale in comparison to the positive impact he had on the American economy as treasury secretary.

In 1921, Mellon took the financial reins of a newly branded federal government. President Woodrow Wilson proclaimed the need for the federal government to be a symbol of democracy. This led to a historic turn that saw an expansion of the federal government. President Wilson justified the implementation of a progressive federal income tax in the name of protecting and spreading American democracy. Under this system, income was charged at different rates depending on how much a person earned. The different income levels were called "tax brackets."

The government saw economic intervention as necessary between the voluntary actions of American business owners and its citizens. When Mellon came into the secretary position, the federal income tax was less than 10 years old. Proponents of the mandated income tax laughed at the idea that any of the tax rates for the different tax brackets could ever get as high as 10 percent. They were so wrong. By 1921, the top income tax bracket was paying 73 percent.

America's founders would be turning in their grave at the idea of a federal income tax for all citizens. The Constitution itself reads, "All duties, imposts and excises shall be uniform throughout the United States." The Fourteenth Amendment solidified the promise of "equal protection of the laws" to all American citizens. This idea of a progressive income tax, "the more you earn, the more you pay," runs directly counter to our founding principles. It allows the government to divide people by creating citizen factions in the name of equality.

Mellon's negative perception of high tax rates was solidified from his father's lessons. He understood his family came to America to escape the crushing burden of overzealous taxes on the people. His father continually reminded him of the principles of free markets throughout his upbringing, because empowering the individual through lower taxes leads to more efficient prosperity for all people. Plus, Mellon himself had first-hand experience with using his wealth for further wealth creation.

What had this new tax burden and mindset of "spreading democracy" brought to America? When Harding wanted Mellon to become the treasury secretary in his cabinet, the United States was facing an economic crisis after World War I, unemployment was up, taxes were rising, and the nation's debt was increasing at an unprecedented rate. In addition to dealing with all of those issues, Mellon would have the task of collecting large loans owed by several European nations for the United States aiding them in WWI.

The national debt was one area of particular concern because of the sheer growth that occurred in less than a decade. From the American Revolution to 1916, the national debt was $1.2 billion. And by the end of World War I, the debt level had ballooned to over $24 billion.

The war debts owed by the European allies for food and war materials further stressed the American economy. The allies owed $10 billion. All sides of the war effort had fallen on hard times from the destructive intrusion of war, so the allied nations became resistant to repayment. Proof that even for the winners, war doesn't pay!

The odds were stacked against Mellon. Few secretaries of the treasury had to overcome such institutional problems facing the United States as he did. President Harding looked to him for financial advice to pull the United States from the grasp of inevitable economic turmoil.

Mellon's plan for saving the American economy was to shrink the size of government. He wanted to pull back the government's hand from the pockets of everyday American citizens and allow them to go back to creating innovative products and solving problems. Luckily for Mellon, he had earned himself an exceptional reputation for his business mindset and, given the difficult times facing the United States, politicians were finally ready to listen.

The plan was to first decrease the United States' debt burden. Mellon was able to renegotiate roughly one-third of the debt at lower interest rates to not only pay it off more quickly but cost the American taxpayer less. Second, he helped cut federal spending from $6.5 billion in 1921 to $2.5 billion in 1926. This way, more funds could be used to pay off the growing debt from before his time as treasury secretary.

After President Harding died in 1923, President Coolidge continued helping Mellon save the American economy by vetoing the legislators "job retention bills" that were just full of special interest legislation that were meant to appeal to voters so specific legislators could be reelected.

Coolidge and Mellon did not believe that extra bonuses to veterans and further subsidies for wheat and cotton farmers were amenities the federal government could afford.

Mellon stayed consistent with his plan to reduce the size of government by cutting staff at the Treasury Department. Helping his plan further, he found a creative way for his department to save money by reducing the physical size of America's paper money. The smaller size of the bills reduced the cost of making new ones, plus the smaller bills were made with more durable paper and better ink, which made them a better alternative for saving money in the long run as well.

Mellon's most important understanding of the American economy might be "that high rates of taxation do not necessarily mean large revenue to the government, and that more revenue may often be obtained by lower rates." As Mellon always did before making a decision, he began researching the problems facing the tax system, along with the negative effects of the high tax rates. He noticed that most wealthy Americans were avoiding paying taxes altogether by finding the vast number of tax loopholes brought about by the complex system caused by high tax rates.

Mellon brought his particular decision-making mindset to his position in the government: bring in information, analyze, and only then make a decision. On the other hand, the government was paying attention to only the outcome of its decision to raise taxes. They only took in part of the information and expected that more taxes should equal more money for the government, because that is how the federal government takes in revenue. Unfortunately, they failed to consider the unintended consequences of business owners taking their business to more friendly locations, seeking tax loopholes, and wasting the resources the rich had to help them find those loopholes. The government failed to properly understand the power of decision making that is widely understood in the world of business: we must consider information that is possibly evidence against the outcome we desire.

After Mellon thoroughly did his research he came up with the idea to cut the top tax rate of 73 percent to 25 percent.

He made it a point to bring his business mindset to his position in the government, understanding the importance of a business-friendly policy to help strengthen the American economy. Being a businessman himself, he knew that large taxes can have devastating effects on a business. Once the regulative and tax burden becomes too great, American business owners are either forced to close down or take their business elsewhere.

Mellon's plan slashed taxes to attract the fortunes back into the American economy. One of his selling points to the federal government was an example from Ford creator, Henry Ford. Ford had figured out he could create more revenue by reducing the price of his cars from $3,000 to $380, understanding that sometimes your earnings can go up by vastly increasing the overall sales. Mellon took this principle to his tax plan by increasing the overall number of taxpayers paying in when compared to the higher "price tag" applied to the wealthiest tax bracket.

What was the result of Mellon cutting spending and making tax cuts across the board? American industries came running back to the safe haven of the United States economy causing an economic boom throughout the 1920s, and unemployment plummeted from 11.7 percent to just 3.3 percent between 1923 and 1929. Even after the tax decreases, tax revenue went from $719 million in 1921 to over $1 billion in 1929, just as Mellon predicted—a well-researched outcome. He also managed to cut the national debt by a quarter.

Mellon's decision-making skills, business mindset, and willingness to take in new information made his plan a glowing success.

Takeaway

Andrew Mellon's story teaches us the importance of consuming a wide variety of information from a wide variety of avenues, be it an inspiring book, a mentor, or the example of a successful parent. He did not allow himself to be blind to information that went against the outcome he desired. This, along with his understanding of the importance of empowering business owners with lower taxes and less regulation, made him the successful businessman and secretary of treasury we remember today. The information and lessons he learned throughout his life helped him reduce government spending, taxation, and our national debt. One thing is clear: his overall mindset is one that we are in dire need of again today.

Fun Facts

- Mellon was an avid art collector, and his art was used to found the National Gallery.

- Although he made more money in oil, he loved the aluminum industry.

- His successful tenure as the Secretary of the Treasury brought talk of a presidential run in 1928. Age kept him on the sidelines.

The world was against me because of my skin color. So I made the best of every opportunity and **changed it.**

Elijah McCOY

Born of fugitive slaves and oppressed at every turn because of the color of his skin, a young boy with a natural curiosity for tinkering overcame all obstacles to become one of the most important inventors of the industrial age.

The Real McCoy

When you want "the real thing" or "the original," you may say you want "the real McCoy." For example, if you wanted the best shoes on the market, not a knock-off, you would walk into the store and proclaim, "I'm looking for the real McCoy."

But wait, whose name was worthy of being attached with such a praiseworthy phrase? Elijah McCoy.

We often hear that it's necessary for public bureaucrats to convince the public that corporations need government handouts to promote economic growth to create progress. However, history tells us a different story. It tells us that when entrepreneurs and inventors are left to their own devices with the freedom to succeed based on their own efforts, we find naturally occurring economic prosperity.

McCoy did just that. Not only did he become a successful inventor thanks to the freedom the market provided, he also destroyed the racist narrative of his time: black people could not compete with whites. His rise to prominence as an inventor came just after the American Civil War. McCoy became a beacon of freedom for people across the world, demonstrating that when we allow all people to experience equal freedom to invent, create and produce in the free market, innovative progress can never be halted.

The Makings of a Creator

McCoy was born in Colchester, Ontario, in 1843. His parents had escaped slavery in Kentucky using the Underground Railroad. Luckily, Canada acted as a sanctuary from the barbarous practices of the United States at the time. This would become beneficial to McCoy's hard-working father, as he was able to make his family economically stable.

McCoy's parents saw potential in him. As a boy, he was always tinkering with his father's tools and machines; he was fascinated by how they worked. He would look at them and analyze how each part came together to make the entire mechanism work. He was forever intrigued!

The success of his father gave his family the resources to send McCoy to an engineering school in Scotland when he was just sixteen. Soon he would go on to earn the credentials of a master mechanic and engineer. After five years of studying mechanical engineering and the end of the American Civil War, McCoy and his family were able to return to the United States safely. They settled in Ypsilanti, Michigan, which was located near the Michigan Central Railroad.

Engineering had become Elijah's passion, and he was ready to take his next step toward becoming the inventor he dreamed of being. Unfortunately, the end of the Civil War did not immediately bring an end to the racial prejudices facing black Americans. McCoy applied to the Central Railroad company as an engineer, but once they discovered he was a black man, they refused to hire him. He was devastated. His work in Scotland had only fueled his passion for understanding the workings of machines, and now cruel and unjust racial profiling was getting in his way.

Although denied the engineering position, he wanted to find a position around the engines as a way to continue to learn and envision innovation. He worked with what he was given. McCoy took a position as a fireman and oilman, which was one of the only railroad positions offered to black Americans at the time.

McCoy gladly took the opportunity. He got his start doing the job nobody else wanted but someone had to do. At the time, around 1870, every moving part in an engine needed to be lubricated with oil, especially the massive steam engine locomotives. The machine could only move as fast as the oilmen could work.

He did his job well, climbing all over the engine to oil every vital part. After several minutes of this undesirable work under the hot machinery, McCoy emerged covered in a dusty glaze of grease and his sweat. His sweat streamed down his face, mixing with oil and coal debris that covered him, stinging his eyes. It was exhausting work.

McCoy was able to visualize the objects around him and make connections to other areas of his life. After putting in backbreaking work to lubricate a train engine, he would emerge and head over to the water bucket to quench his thirst. After doing this repeatedly, he began to notice the similarity between the train and himself: both he and the train needed to replenish with liquids to keep everything running smoothly. He needed water, while the machine needed oil.

Finding a Solution

Have you ever noticed your parent's car dinging to let them know it requires an oil change? If you put off getting that oil change, the moving parts of your car will get extra hot! In time, your engine will begin running less efficiently, and engine parts may corrode, warp, and wear out. Eventually, your engine will need to be replaced!

Luckily, the innovative power of the free market has not only brought us automobiles to drive wherever we need to go, but it also opened up a service opportunity for businesses as well. With cars requiring tune-ups and oil changes, mechanics shops exist within a few mile radius of almost everyone in the United States.

Imagine the locomotive steam engine of McCoy's time. These large engines needed workers to lubricate the moving parts of the machine manually. The steam power caused higher pressure and considerably more heat, making the conditions ruthlessly corrosive to the metal on the locomotive. The oil provided a thin layer of lubrication to help protect the steam cylinders and pistons.

The engines didn't have a self-lubricating system that we see today. Now, we pour oil into a car and the mechanism is in place to properly lubricate everything needed on your vehicle, like magic! Due to the trains being in constant need of lubrication, they needed to make regular stops on the journey. If the trains didn't stop, it would cause overheating and fires in the engine. But stopping too often caused freights and passengers to become delayed—stifling the railroad system with inefficiency.

McCoy recognized this inefficiency. Since he was a child, his mind was always turning, imagining what he could do to make things more efficient. With his lifetime of experience, he was able to identify the problem: someone needed to find a way to lubricate the steam engine while the train was still in motion.

He immediately set to work on the problem after his shifts as an oilman. After tinkering, testing, and rethinking his invention, he had made the perfect prototype of a lubricating cup. His device used a reservoir of oil that gradually fed the oil to the various parts that needed lubrication, doing all of this while the locomotive was still in motion. Although this new mechanical invention of his would make his own job obsolete, he saw it as a risk worth taking. His mind was made for creating.

Once McCoy had successfully created the lubricating cup, word of his creation spread. Railroad companies and conductors did everything they could to get their hands on one. This new invention fixed the problem at hand, kept the trains on a more accurate schedule, and made cargo deliveries quicker and more reliable. Additionally, passengers on the trains were glad to arrive at their destinations quicker. Everyone was happy! Business was booming!

Demand for McCoy's invention skyrocketed. There was one problem, though: McCoy didn't have time to create an infrastructure to build his new invention fast enough, and the free market would not wait for him. Imitations of his invention began popping up across the country to fill this new market gap.

However, while others tried to copy his invention, none of these imitations could meet the golden standard that McCoy's version had achieved. His attention to detail, engineering skills, and standard of quality was so high that his lubrication cup was what all the railroad companies wanted on their steam engines, and they were willing to pay top dollar.

To avoid confusion around the other various lubrication

cups on the market, railroad businessmen and owners started asking for "the real McCoy." This was the birth of the famous phrase, but steam engine lubrication was not McCoy's only invention. It was only the beginning.

Takeaway

McCoy's invention had a ripple effect on the locomotive industry. With lubrication made easier and corrosive effects much less of an issue, it created an opportunity for innovation of the steam engine itself. They were soon able to run faster and, by consequence, hotter. This created another opportunity for Elijah to continue enhancing his creations; it was a chance to benefit the market and the people. He went on to create a graphite/oil lubricator made just for this issue.

Success would continue to follow him. He was a man looking to solve problems. He viewed everything with a lens of wonder. He was always asking himself "what can I do to make this better?" This question led him to patent fifty-seven inventions in his productive life. A few of his accomplishments were his enhanced lubricator cup, an improved air brake lubricator, and an enhanced wheel tire. He was filing patents into his 70s. His mind never stopped looking to improve. In 1920, he founded the Elijah McCoy Manufacturing Company in Detroit, a fantastic accomplishment for the time period given the prejudices of the times. He continued to create until his death in 1929 at the age of 86.

McCoy is a beautiful symbol of the power of free markets. After the Civil War, a time when people were free from the shackles of overregulation by the hands of government—

the rise of the regulatory state wouldn't come for another century—they were free to create. This included the finally free black Americans. This free enterprise of our country's past allowed black Americans to show white people the creative power they, too, possess.

McCoy took this opportunity and cemented his name in history for perfecting creations in a way that nobody else could.

Fun Facts

- After perfecting the lubricating cup for locomotive railroad engines, his designs made their way to ship engines.

- Elijah considered his engine lubricator combo his greatest invention. It decreased the use of coal and oil.

When something is important enough, you do it even if the odds are not in your favor.

Elon MUSK

He's tenacious… maybe even reckless with his drive to transform the world. So what makes Elon different from others with a similar vision? He's smart and bold enough to follow through.

To do:
- *Make payments easy on-line.* ✓
- *Make cars electric.* ✓
- *Power the world with the sun.* ✓
- *Make cars drive themselves.* ✓
- *Build a colony on Mars.*

"I try to do useful things… That's a nice aspiration. And useful means it is of value to the rest of society. Are they useful things that work and make people's lives better, make the future seem better, and actually are better too? I think we should try to make the future better."

A Modern Innovator

Today, Elon Musk is one of the most recognizable names in the world. His groundbreaking innovations place him at the forefront of technologies from electric cars to space travel and have established his place in history as one of the most innovative tech tycoons. He is driven by his passion to save mankind from possible destruction.

Every entrepreneur has to have a driving principle. For Musk, that passion is saving and protecting the human race.

There is a modern misconception in the media that entrepreneurship is all about making money, and that business is inherently full of greedy people. Many look at free market capitalism with a narrow scope, only picking out the pieces of information that fit their narrative. They want to see the world as full of evil businessmen who only want to collect money and stockpile it.

That's far from the truth.

Musk has a framed poster in his office with the saying, "When you wish upon a falling star, your dreams can come true. Unless it's really a meteor hurtling to the Earth which will destroy all life. Then you're pretty much hosed, no matter what you wish for. Unless it's death by meteorite." At first glance, this quote appears to be a well-played attempt at dark humor, but for Musk to have this in his office tells a different story.

Elon Musk doesn't just wish and dream; he tries to make a change!

His desire to save humanity has made him notorious for setting unrealistic goals, which has been followed with unattainable workloads and the verbal abuse of employees. This point needs to be known, as Musk is notorious for taking on a draining schedule.

On Monday, he is at SpaceX in Los Angeles until Tuesday night. On Wednesdays and Thursdays, he goes to Silicon Valley to be at Tesla. Then he heads back to Los Angeles for more tasks to finish out the week. He is relentless in his work to make his visions become a reality.

The New York Times called Musk "arguably the most successful and important entrepreneur in the world." He is also the only person to start four billion-dollar companies: PayPal, Tesla, SpaceX, and Solar City.

A Child with a Knack for Wisdom

Elon Musk grew up in South Africa and was a young genius from the start. At the age of 12, he developed and sold a video game called Blastar for $500. Although stories like this have become much more commonplace with today's generation growing up during the tech craze, at the time of Musk's childhood this was something special.

His childhood was not easy. He was severely bullied; he was always the youngest and smallest kid in the class. This made it difficult for Musk to make friends in school, and his parents did not provide a loving home life. His parents divorced and Musk chose to live with his father. This is a decision he regrets today, as he was bullied both at school and at home by his father. Musk needed an outlet for his time. He turned to reading, studying, and theorizing about the world.

A major influence on Musk was Isaac Asimov's Foundation series of books. The series focuses on studying patterns of the past to predict the future. This introduced Musk to a new way of using the scientific method. Of course he had heard of this method of thinking in the many science books he read. But using it as an innovative tool for thinking about the future was something different. The series had Musk truly looking to the stars for answers.

Gathering knowledge from books is a practice Musk continues to this day. During his younger years, he read two books a day! He makes it a point to gather knowledge from as many areas as possible, spanning from science fiction, physics, philosophy, religion, biographies, entrepreneurs, technology, marketing, and psychology. His areas of interest are endless.

Musk applies information he learned in one area of interest to others. For example, he might take a future-focused idea found in science fiction and apply it to what he knows about physics. This allows him to think beyond what most people believe to be possible. The thought process can lead to real-world groundbreaking solutions!

As Musk found solace in his books, he realized something else: he could remember everything he read. He had a photographic memory that allowed him to memorize the multitude of books he was consuming. The way his mind operated, he saw that answering questions is the easy part. If he learned the proper material, he could answer a question. But, Musk realized that the important thing to do is ask the right questions.

Asking the right questions allows you to find new and improved answers because answering questions is easy; it's finding new questions that need to be answered that's harder. The ability to answer questions that nobody else is asking gives you the opportunity to solve problems that nobody thought of solving.

Luckily for Musk, free enterprise is always looking for innovative problem solvers.

A Real-Life Tony Stark

Musk attended a few universities during his college years, but his brilliant mind left him feeling bored and unchallenged. After earning his degree in physics from the Wharton School, he began a PhD program at Stanford University. He stayed for two days before dropping out to pursue his real vision and ambition—entrepreneurship.

In 1995, Musk and his brother founded Zip2. They sold it for $307 million. In 1999, he went on to co-found X.com, which came out on the forefront of online banking services. A year later the company merged with the still widely used payment service PayPal. However, Musk left the company in 2000 because the merged companies would not allow him the decision making power he desired. These companies were stepping stones towards Musk's true creative desires. And luckily for him, he left PayPal with stock options worth $180 million to help make those dreams become a reality.

Musk knew exactly what steps he wanted to take next. He put $100 million into starting SpaceX, then $70 million into starting Tesla, and finally invested the remaining $10 million in Solar City.

He was a man on a mission.

The Mindset of a Billionaire

First-principles thinking is an idea that many aspiring entrepreneurs have studied religiously. A simple understanding of this mindset popularized by Musk is to get your mind to a clean state to act as a starting point to think about solving a problem. Having a clear mind during a problem-solving process can have endless benefits when thinking about valuable solutions to the issues facing society!

Take a moment and imagine a rocket in front of you. Now recognize what you think of when you look at the rocket. Maybe it's something along the lines of, 'Wow that's really cool,' 'How do I launch it?' or 'How do I make it blow something up?' But, now, put your entrepreneur hat on to get your mind into innovation mode. For Musk, he looks at what a rocket is made of, understanding the aerospace-grade aluminum alloys, titanium, copper, and carbon fiber. He would then price out all of those products with the quantity needed to determine if making his own would be cheaper than buying on the open market. He would then find the material cost of the rocket was two percent of the asking price of a completed rocket. Boom, he found an opportunity!

After he made these deductions, SpaceX was born.

The market does not always demand that a creator reinvent the wheel. Sometimes it's best to improve upon it, make it more efficient, or make it cheaper with better quality. First-principles thinking is a useful method that helps us take the blinders off of our minds to discover new perspectives.

It's an important mindset because humans often make up their minds about something and refuse to change it, even when new counter-evidence is brought before them. This is extremely problematic when you're trying to find entrepreneurial opportunities. You won't create a startup as successful as PayPal if you assume the market is already creating the best, most efficient, and cheapest products in every area of life!

In an interview with Rolling Stone, Elon Musk laid out his first-principles thinking method:

1. Ask a question.

2. Gather as much evidence as possible about it.

3. Develop facts based on the evidence and try to assign a probability of truth to each one.

4. Draw a conclusion based on cogency in order to determine: Are these facts correct? Are they relevant? Do they necessarily lead to this conclusion, and with what probability?

5. Attempt to disprove the conclusion. Seek refutation from others to further help break your conclusion.

6. If nobody can invalidate your conclusion, then you're probably right, but you're not certainly right.

For Musk, his first principles thinking became fundamental to his worldview and provided him a mindset for finding potential markets in a free enterprise system. Essentially, the idea behind first principles thinking is boiling down situations in life to their individual parts. This is crucial for understanding concepts and making decisions based on the information gathered. Overall, it's a wonderful thinking tool to become an innovative entrepreneur and find potential gaps in the market. It then helps you understand how to attack the situation with precision.

Another important aspect of this mindset, in relation to entrepreneurialism, is it can help take out the emotion involved in your decision-making process. Many people with entrepreneurial ambitions have the desire to believe their "innovative" solution will succeed. But humans fear failure, leading to many creators having their minds trick them into wishful thinking. Wishful thinking does not equal results. Using first principles thinking before you make important decisions will allow you to determine the best decision because you have gone through the proper thinking process to gather the necessary information.

An essential aspect of becoming an innovator is to have a creative mindset. With that creative mindset, you need a reason-based decision-making process, which is what first principles thinking provides.

But maybe most of all, just remember to love the process of learning!

The Tax Money Entrepreneur

Although Musk's life undoubtedly provides many lessons that young entrepreneurs can learn from, he also sheds light on the growing issue of crony capitalism here in America. The government should not be in the business of picking winners and losers, and in the case of Elon Musk, his more recent ventures have been propped up by tax dollars while Musk maintains the guise of functioning in the private sector.

One of the few government spending cuts performed by President Obama was cuts to the NASA space program. To help maintain a presence in space, NASA contracted out to private companies to help carry cargo and astronauts to the International Space Station. This is where Musk's SpaceX came to the rescue, helpfully using their new spacecraft and rockets to be more involved in government space programs.

NASA was only funding near-Earth voyages, but that only scratched the surface of Musk's space exploration ambitions. The near-Earth space travel contracts were already becoming mired in government inefficiency, but even knowing that the government's involvement in the process brought waste along with it, SpaceX still wanted NASA to form a partnership with them to fund deep space voyages at the expense of the taxpayer.

In total, Musk's various billion-dollar companies have received $4.9 billion in government subsidies. Although he remains an innovative mind and someone to take many lessons from analyzing the world around us, his experience demonstrates the problems inherent with tying your company to government funding.

This is a reminder that even the greatest entrepreneurial minds will look for handouts to fund the experiments they are not willing to fund on their own.

Takeaway

Love him or hate him, the man who is often considered the real-life Tony Stark for his can-do attitude and innovative companies will be remembered in history for many generations to come. He is someone who prides himself on finding solutions that he thinks are valuable for society. Although we might disagree with his over-reliance on government subsidies, we cannot deny his desire to help improve the world.

And we must recognize the areas where Elon Musk has found success: he never stops learning, is still trying to bring in new information that attacks his own worldview, and is willing to accept the possibility of being wrong. The openness to learning and the desire to find solutions to the problems of the world has led to his contributions to humanity.

But maybe the most important takeaway is that even though Elon Musk is one of a kind, the tools he used to find success in the world are open to all.

Fun Facts

- Musk read an entire encyclopedia series at the age of 9.

- Musk had one of his companies create a modern flamethrower… because why not?

- Robert Downey Jr, who played Ironman, sat down with Musk to get inspiration for his character Tony Stark.

A good reputation is measured by how much you can improve the lives of others.

George
EASTMAN

It's hard to imagine a world without photographs, but until relatively recently, the only images from the past were the ones from memory. The invention of cameras changed all that, and it's because of Eastman that these miraculous tools became available and affordable to virtually everyone.

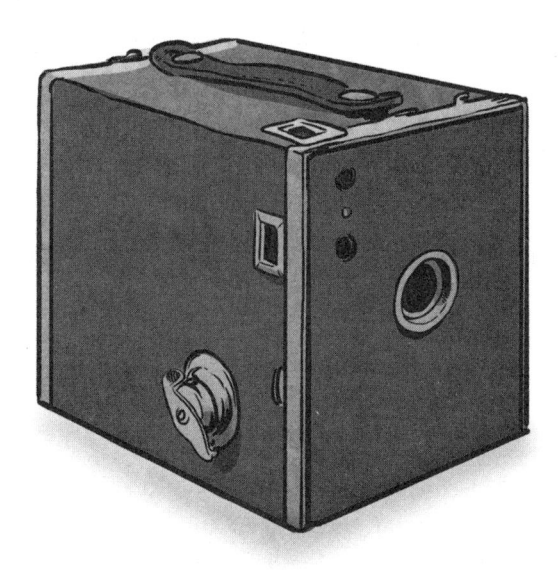

"What we do during our working hours determines what we have; what we do in our leisure hours determines what we are."

An Inventor of Passion

Think of what your life would be like without photos of your past. Or ask yourself what would it be like to be unable to see events from around the world in the newspaper or online?

We often forget about the powerful minds, inventors, and entrepreneurs who helped pave the way for the great innovations we use in our lives today. George Eastman was one of those great minds. As an entrepreneur, he brought the power of photography within reach of everyday Americans when such a feat seemed impossible.

Eastman was born in the quaint village of Waterville, New York, on July 12, 1854. At just five years old, his father sold his small nursery business to move the family to Rochester, New York, to open Eastman Commercial College. Shortly after the move, his father died, leaving eight-year-old George and his family with massive financial problems, as well as a newly established college whose success would prove to be short-lived.

When Eastman turned 14, his family's dwindling finances forced him to drop out of school and quickly find employment to support his widowed mother and two sisters, one of whom suffered from polio. Eastman knew he had no other choice.

As a teenager, Eastman was lucky to find an office job with an insurance company. From one small pay raise to the next, he slowly worked his way up the income chain, but it was still not enough for his family's expenses. He began to study accounting in his spare time, taking on the extra stress to qualify for a better paying position at the company. Five years of hard work and dedication finally paid off when he was hired as a junior clerk in 1874 at Rochester Savings Bank.

In the same year, Eastman found himself becoming fascinated with photography—a technology that was still in its infancy.

He began to focus his interest on this new technology. He understood that a good entrepreneur must remain curious about the world around them, always looking for opportunities to improve the world by serving others through problem-solving.

With an explorative soul and growing interest in photography, Eastman began to plan a trip to Santo Domingo, a beautiful city on the coast of the Dominican Republic. He wanted to capture the city's charm and preserve it on film forever. He excitedly gathered up his photography supplies in preparation, including a photographic outfit, or "hauling camera," and soon realized that hauling around all the bulky equipment required for photography at the time made it unsuitable for most travelers. According to Eastman's personal account, the camera required "a pack-horse load" of gear and supplies. Can you imagine carrying that by yourself on your next hike? He canceled the trip in frustration. But his frustration served an important purpose: it ignited a dream of creating travel-friendly photographic technology. Eastman had found his passion.

Eastman had become accustomed to the bulky, unreliable cameras of his time that needed various liquids to function and a tripod to hold them up, but realized that the size and amount of equipment needed for photography made it impractical. In the 1870s, cameras were the size of a microwave oven. He recognized that others must be as frustrated with the size of the equipment as he was.

Eastman also realized the beauty in being able to make moments last forever in a photograph. He wanted to introduce the beauty of photography to the masses.

For Eastman, it wasn't just about the photographs; it was about seeing the joy others experienced from taking and viewing photographs. Following his canceled trip, he decided he no longer wanted to just accept the way things were. By solving his own problems with photography, many other people would benefit, too. From that point on, he was dedicated to finding a way to simplify the entire photo taking process.

The Inventor

Eastman recognized that the liquid chemicals required for photography were a significant strain on photographers—an obstacle that certainly needed an alternative. Photographers had to carry around jugs of the substances which they had to quickly apply to develop the photographs after the picture was captured. This problem had no easy solution, especially for a man working full time at a bank to provide for his family. Nevertheless, he worked tirelessly through many long nights experimenting and formulating solutions in his mother's kitchen.

By 1880, after three difficult years of experimentation, long hours, and financial risk, Eastman had finally discovered a way to print photos using a dry-chemical formula. There was no longer a need for the heavy, sloppy and cumbersome chemicals used in wet-plate photography.

Eastman quickly recognized the untapped business potential for his new invention. He had to consider the possibility of financial ruin as he left the security of a paycheck in pursuit of his dreams. He had to entertain the possibility of creating a successful invention, only to have the public not buy it.

But Eastman was ready to take on these risks. He was prepared to embrace an entrepreneurial mindset for a product he believed in, and one he knew the public would love. He took a leap of faith by quitting his banking job to fully dedicate himself to his new photography company: Eastman Dry Plate Company of Rochester New York. With his experimental mindset and new technology at hand, he created a patented machine to prepare large numbers of photographic plates.

This was a different period in America; taxes were low, and the government stayed clear of meddling in the works of creative minds. This setting allowed George to continue his efforts to accomplish his dreams. For a high school dropout who was once labeled "not especially gifted," George had come a long way.

"What we were doing was not merely making dry plates, but that we were starting out to make photography an everyday affair."

"Kodak Freaks"

As Eastman's dry-plate business grew, so did his fame. He became a household name within the photography community—a man who had revolutionized the visual arts. But he was far from done. Simplifying the photography chemical process was a great achievement, but he still saw problems with the equipment itself, which was still large and burdensome to use. Throughout the 1880s, he experimented with alternative materials to reduce the size of the necessary equipment, looking to provide a portable camera option.

By 1888, Eastman's hard work paid off yet again. He created a camera that was smaller, cheaper, and more straightforward—the first Kodak camera. This simple camera fit into a handheld box measuring less than 4 inches high and six and a half inches long. The camera used roll film technology capable of 100 exposures. Once the roll was filled, the customer sent the film to the Eastman Dry Plate Company. They developed the film and sent it back to the customer. Although Eastman had no previous marketing experience, he understood the importance of advertising and promptly formulated a recognizable and catchy campaign for his new camera: "You press the button. We do the rest!" It was another risk, as his company was taking on the labor cost to develop these films and relying on the customer to continue buying more, but this venture ultimately proved to be successful as well.

Eastman's desire for innovation didn't stop there. He con tinued to apply his experience and skills to simplify photography for the average person. For instance, he designed a more flexible film that could be inserted and taken out of the camera more efficiently than the traditional system. These developments were eventually picked up by Thomas Edison who used the film in the first motion-picture camera—a contribution which went far beyond Eastman's initial use.

But Eastman hadn't yet fully achieved his dream. He wanted the art of photography to be accessible for every individual. Even though he had made significant progress by making his Kodak cameras smaller and cheaper than cameras had ever been before, it still cost $25, or about $500 in today's dollars. At the time, this was unaffordable to most people. Eastman and his team went back to the drawing board to achieve what would be their most significant feat yet: cutting cost while also improving the quality of their cameras.

Once again, Eastman overcame the issue he set about to solve. The Kodak Brownie camera was released in 1900 with a $1 price tag. It was finally possible for almost anyone to capture memories with ease. Eastman's innovations forever cemented him in history as the founder of the amateur photography craze that is still growing today.

Eastman's new high quality, inexpensive camera flew off the shelves. He was finally bringing his dream into reality. Millions of people were caught up in the craze. A 1905 report coined the phrase "Kodak Freaks," referring to the movement of people taking their Brownie cameras everywhere to capture experiences and preserve memories.

Eastman lived during a period when owning a photograph of your family was an expensive, rare, and special thing. He changed all of that, creating the first wave of amateur photographers looking to capture many different moments in time. Finally, photographs were at the stage where they could become mementos to look back on to relive the important moments of our lives.

His inventions revolutionized how we thought about photography and preserving memories. Eastman opened the door for people to start preserving their stories and more easily share those precious moments with others. Future inventors built on his ideas and developed the technology that we take for granted today that enables us to carry a high-quality camera right in our pocket to use at our convenience.

More than Just an Inventor and Businessman

Throughout many years of hard work and dedication, George Eastman maintained a consistent philosophy in all areas of his life. He never pursued his desire for accessible photography for the sake of making money; that was more of an intended consequence. He had a bigger dream in mind. Consider the success of his first Kodak camera: rather than quitting and keeping his profits after his first major success, he kept going. He used the funds to continue his research toward a better and cheaper camera. He was on an unstoppable journey to make photography accessible to everyone—a dream that money alone would simply not fulfill.

Eastman's generosity was apparent through his inventions, business, and philanthropic efforts. He was one of the first American industrialists to incorporate employee profit sharing, where he would gift his own money to each of his workers. His generosity didn't stop at his business ventures, as he gave millions to the Rochester Institute of Technology and Massachusetts Institute of Technology, along with various other educational institutions. The "progress of the world depends almost entirely upon education," he once said.

By 1924 Eastman had given away half of his fortune—an estimated $100 million in donations throughout his lifetime. He funded various industries including education, health, teaching, and the arts.

Choosing His Own Path

Eastman started his life with nothing and was still able to achieve his dream of creating something valuable while sharing his generosity with others. No one told him what to do or how to do it. He lived his life according to his own passions and merits, creating a unique path along the way.

The power of the free market helped pave the way for Eastman to identify a problem in society and look to provide an answer himself. He was left free from overbearing regulations and incentives from politicians and bureaucrats. While many modern industries rely on monetary incentives from the government to jump-start their businesses, Eastman took his own financial risks, using his personal time and money to ensure success for his revolutionary camera.

When it came to Eastman's employees, he did not need the government to mandate what he paid them; he paid them well, based on their value to the company. Most importantly, he did not need the government to force him to use his fortune to give back; he chose to donate to other people's visions that he believed in.

George Eastman's story teaches us to cultivate the drive to create, innovate, and help others. It was the freedom of an entrepreneur and inventor, not government planners, that revolutionized picture taking. He started a foundation for the future of photography motion pictures. His love of capturing memories gave him the drive to put this feeling of joy into the hands of the everyday person by making expensive technologies accessible to everyone. The freedom Eastman enjoyed allowed him to improve the lives of people for generations to come.

Fun Facts

- Even though Eastman invented amateur photography, he didn't go out of his way to be photographed. There are actually few photographs of him.

- He would often go unrecognized in his hometown of Rochester in which he played an integral part in creating the thriving community.

- Eastman never married, claiming he was "too busy" and "too poor" during his younger years.

An ordinary gift to be bragged about is not a gift in the eyes of the Lord.

Hetty
GREEN

In an age when it was uncommon for a woman to be involved in business at all, Hetty became a master of it. Using the knowledge of finance she learned from her father, and the wisdom and frugality of her Quaker heritage, she became the richest woman in the world.

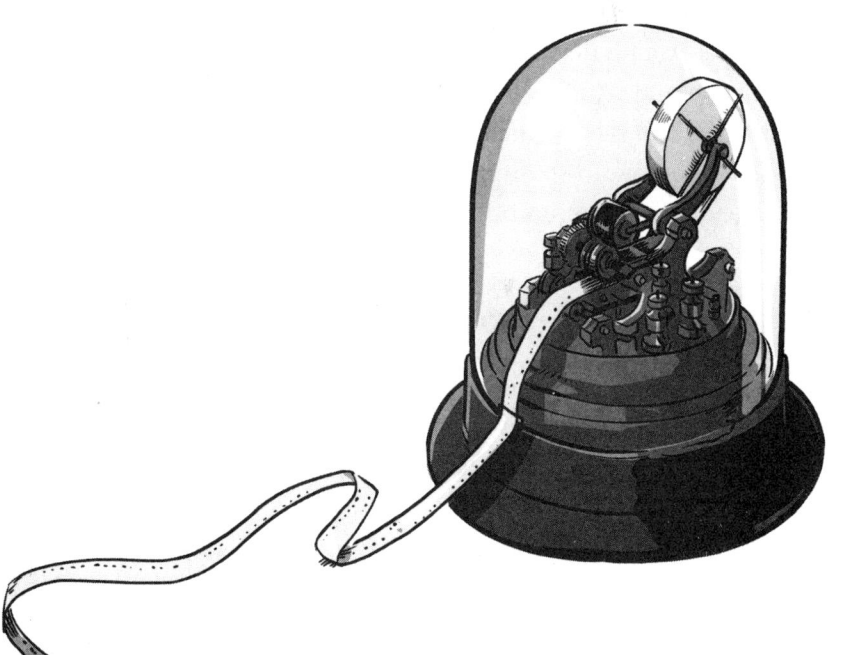

"In this way I came to know what stocks and bonds were, how the markets fluctuated, and the meaning of bulls and bears."

The Witch of Wall Street

Banks are businesses that accept deposits, distribute loans, and derive profit from the interest on those loans. All banks have a company structure of employees, managers, and board of directors.

However, sometimes people become so smart with their money that they become a bank themselves—a one-person bank. Henrietta Howland Robinson Green was one such person. She was commonly known as Hetty Green, or the Witch of Wall Street.

In today's society, many would have us believe that the rich stockpile their money and leave it sitting around, but the opposite is true. If those with lots of money were to leave it sitting around doing nothing, the pile would begin getting smaller and smaller. In order for entrepreneurs to increase their pile of money, they must reinvest their money into the economy. This also stimulates the economy and creates economic growth for others to enjoy.

Upbringing

Green was born into a Quaker family of whale hunters in New Bedford, Massachusetts, in 1834. You could say she was made for the financial world from birth. She was reading finance strategy papers to her father and grandfather at the age of six! She had the foresight to not merely read the papers, though. She internalized and understood the information as she read.

Her grandfather, Gideon Howland, encouraged all of his

grandchildren to read the latest financial news from books to newspapers. He was trying to make them prepared and knowledgeable about all things pertaining to the financial world. Hetty's grandfather and father acted as mentors about the ins and outs of the financial world. For them, finance was the real land of opportunity, and they wanted Green to be ready when opportunities presented themselves. This was a skill that would benefit Hetty in the future.

Her only brother died very young, leaving Hetty the heir to the large family fortune. Luckily, her parents and grandparents understood that women could handle the financial world just as well as men could, as long as they were willing to put in the time to educate themselves. Her family understood that your ability to excel in the financial world wasn't about which gender you are, it's about being willing to learn and take advantage of an opportunity. The important key was to have a better grasp of the principles of the financial world than everyone else. And that's exactly what Green aspired to do!

Although she had learned the ins and outs of finance through her childhood, her father was still set in his traditional ways: Green was to find an upstanding husband. Her father bought her a set of new dresses to attract a wealthy husband. However, she had other plans in mind for the dresses. She sold them in order to buy bonds with the revenue.

Green was always looking for ways to spread around her wealth! She lived by her own rules. She was trained to pursue her own personal self-interest, and she did just that.

Money Makes Money

Green trusted her knowledge and handled her own finances. She had the courage to act on the decisions she made and was willing to accept the consequences that came with it. Her mistakes and victories would be her own.

She bought and sold real estate, railroads, and even city blocks. She owned various businesses and held mortgages on everything from churches to large factories. New York City even came to her more than once in need of a loan and for financial advice.

Green helped make significant progress in transforming the narrative about women in business. During her time, it was believed that women did not belong in the business world because they didn't have the mind for it; however, she showed that women were capable of being wise investors. Green was able to become one of the richest people of her time.

Though she was very successful, Green did have faults people can learn from. For instance, she had a reputation for being extremely miserly in her personal life. In one instance, she refused to pay doctors 50 cents to fix her 14-year-old son's dislocated knee. Eventually, gangrene set in on her son's leg. During this time, gangrene was no joking matter, and because she hadn't paid for his care when the injury was new, it made the problem worse. Eventually, her son's leg needed to be amputated. This is a helpful reminder that we sometimes need to check our initial reaction and be willing to act when wisdom requires it.

Although Green was using her wealth to create opportunities for others, which ultimately led to a better lifestyle for many, she needed to act with more wisdom in her personal life. Part of having a stable financial situation is creating a happier personal life for yourself and those around you—especially your family.

As a relatively quiet woman, known as being stingy with her money to a fault, people came to call her a "mean old woman" with too much money and too small of a heart.

This *New York Times* editorial after her death in 1916 sums up Hetty Green well:

> "If a man had lived as did Mrs. Hetty Green, devoting the greater part of his time and mind to the increasing of an inherited fortune that even at the start was far larger than is needed for the satisfaction of all such human needs as money can satisfy, nobody would have seen him as very peculiar—as notably out of the common.

> He would have done what is expected of the average man so circumscribed, and there would have been no difficulty in understanding the joys he obtained from participation in the grim conflicts of higher finance. It was the fact that Mrs. Green was a woman that made her career the subject of endless curiosity, comment and astonishment… [S]he had enough courage to live as she chose and to be as thrifty as she pleased and she observed such of the world's conventions as seemed to her right and useful, coldly and calmly ignoring all the others."

Takeaway

Green became an example for today's financial gurus. She grew her fortune from investing in real estate, stocks, and bonds. She knew how to properly study business models and make optimal business decisions. Part of this understanding was knowing how to locate the value in a business or real estate location and to take a vested interest in seeing the project through.

Also, her understanding of money helped her see the importance of spreading her wealth. In a truly free market economy, it's important to use your money to make more money. This allows your wealth to create more value for society as a whole. Through her investments, Green was able to provide locations for people to start businesses, provide job opportunities for many citizens, and fund innovation. Her wise investments created opportunities for progress for the American people. Everyone wins!

Often, the government doesn't have a vested interest in seeing a project through. When the government makes a mistake, they often just throw more money at the problem. However, financial investors like Green have a personal interest in seeing their investments succeed, which creates a personal concern for efficiency and quality.

Fun Fact

- Some of her popular nicknames were "America's first female tycoon," "The World's Greatest Miser," and "The scrooge of scrooges."

Dreams **can** come true, but success is not an entitlement. It has to be earned every day.

Howard SCHULTZ

Not so long ago, there weren't many things more boring than a cup of coffee. But when Howard discovered what high quality coffee smelled and tasted like, his passion led him to want to share it with everyone. Getting a cup of coffee these days feels like a cultural experience thanks to his efforts.

"Don't let anyone, even your mom and dad, tell you that your dreams cannot come true... They can, but success is not an entitlement. It has to be earned every day."

Acting on a Vision

When you hear someone say "Starbucks," what comes to mind? You probably immediately think of coffee, or maybe the familiar coffee smell of a Starbucks location. Perhaps you see tables full of people working on their laptops or a couple on a coffee date. No matter what comes to mind, everyone is likely to know precisely what you're talking about, even if they don't drink coffee!

The brand recognition that Starbucks has achieved is transforming America's understanding of what it means to get a coffee. The credit for this goes to the company's leader, Howard Schultz.

The Start

Schultz was born in 1953. From the time he was three, his family lived in a small apartment in a rough neighborhood in Brooklyn, New York. Both of his parents struggled to find work. His father was a World War II veteran who jumped from job to job as a low paid laborer; his mother had a similar fate as a low paid receptionist.

Schultz describes his relationship with his father as "complicated." Although he had a rough upbringing with two parents living paycheck to paycheck, witnessing the struggles they went through provided him with useful life lessons that would stay with him into adulthood.

Howard remembered one time in particular of his father lying on their living room couch: distressed, disheartened, and beaten. At the time, Howard's father had a job delivering cloth diapers. But while his father was out on a delivery on a cold winter day in Brooklyn, he slipped and fell on a patch of ice, breaking his hip and ankle. With his father unable to perform his job, he was let go by his employer. This put Howard's family in further distress; they were struggling to make ends meet. For months following, his family was scraping to put food on the table. This experience influenced the life of young Schultz. It left him imagining a better life for himself, and he acted on that vision to work toward a better future.

With all the uneasiness going on in the Shultz household, Howard needed an escape. He found it in sports. Whether it was at school or the neighborhood playgrounds, sports fed his competitive spirit and took his mind off the stresses of home. After graduating from high school, something neither of his parents had been able to do, he made his way to Northern Michigan University with hopes of earning a football scholarship. Unfortunately, it never happened. However, Howard decided to stick with his plan of graduating from college; it was a goal he made for himself. His mind was determined!

He decided to stay at NMU and work his way through college with part-time jobs and some student loans. In 1975, he became the first in his family to graduate from college. His vision for the future was ready for the next stage.

The Power of Determination

Schultz decided to jump right into marketing and sales. He always envisioned himself as someone who had the mindset and determination to take a product to the next level of success. But first, he knew he had to develop his skills to make that vision a reality. His first job after college was selling office equipment door-to-door. It was a sales job, requiring cold calls, talking with potential clients, and marketing the product given to him. It was perfect practice for his dream.

He made sure to remember his upbringing by paying respect to his parents. While at his first job, he sent half of his paychecks home to his parents to help them to pay bills as they grew older. After jumping from sales job to sales job and continuing to gather valuable experience, he found a job at a home appliance store. This would end up being a pivot point for Schultz: the light-bulb moment for moving to the next level of his vision.

While working there, a small coffee company in Seattle, Washington, caught Schultz's eye. They focused on selling high-quality coffee beans. At the time, coffee was not generally consumed throughout the day. It was mainly drunk at breakfast. He was curious about their customer base, so he decided to visit the small company.

The three founders of Starbucks were not young, aspiring entrepreneurs. Jerry Baldwin and Zev Siegl were both teachers and Gordon Bowker was a writer. They were unique because they weren't driven to grow their business. They merely wanted to sell high-quality coffee, because that's what they loved.

When Schultz walked into the small Starbucks storefront, he was immediately hit with the aroma of freshly brewed coffee, a delightful smell to his nose and mind. The store had passed the smell test, but of central importance was the taste. He grabbed himself a cup, and was instantly hooked. He knew that this store was unique. He had a feeling that he had found the product to match his vision.

"When I walked in this store for the first time," he said, "I knew I was home."

Schultz asked the owners for a job as their head of marketing and advertising. Initially, they declined. They thought he had too many ideas and was too eager to make drastic changes. However, Schultz was relentless. He had set his mind on joining the Starbucks team. He called and told Baldwin he was making a huge mistake. This made Baldwin pause. He was struck by Schultz's genuine energy and passion for their product. A few months later, the partners offered Schultz a position, and he was ready to seize the opportunity! It wasn't long before he was a part owner in the business.

Understanding the Coffee Experience

In 1983, Schultz took a trip to Italy to attend an international business conference. While there, he noticed the people walking around the streets of their cities. It was a relaxing practice, a way to get some fresh air and enjoy the beautiful architecture surrounding them. Howard took an opportunity during a conference break to stroll the streets of Italy. He noticed something unique, something not found in the United States at the time: coffee shops on every corner.

But it wasn't the number of coffee shops on the streets that captivated Schultz, it was the aroma of high-quality coffee and the feeling of community the streets provided. He realized that Italy provided an experience along with your coffee drink of choice. The coffee shops offered an inviting atmosphere, places to sit outside, and the presence of other people laughing and talking. It was a complete coffee *experience*. He was hooked. He had found a bold business vision to bring back to the States.

At the time, in the United States, the trend for "getting coffee" was to do it as quickly as possible. Get in, get your coffee, get out to move onto the next task. Schultz changed that idea of "getting coffee" forever.

His aim was to encourage customers to take the time to enjoy the coffee.

Upon his return to Seattle, Schultz was energized to market his new vision. He walked into the small coffee shop ready to discuss his plan with the other owners. Although by now, Starbucks had expanded so that they were serving coffee at a small chain of stores, the staple of the business was still the sales of the coffee beans. Prepared coffee itself was mostly used as a way for people to sample the beans. Howard was ready to take the store on to something more; however, the owners were not.

The business divided into two sides: Schultz wanted to expand the product offerings, one of them being a coffee experience, while the other owners wanted to continue to focus on selling coffee beans. Luckily for Schultz, being a part owner provided him leverage to incorporate some of his ideas in one of the stores. In 1984, he was able to open a small espresso bar in the back of a store. It was a great success. Customers were starting to walk in for a cup of coffee, not to buy the beans. Still, he felt like he'd only been able to test out a shell of his overall vision. More steps were needed, and he was ready to take his next big leap.

Even after the continued success of the espresso bar, the other owners continued to push back. Both sides had their own visions which was preventing the business from moving forward. Schultz knew he needed to step aside in order to progress. He had been convinced that his vision would work from the feedback he was receiving from the successful small coffee bar. That was enough information to take a reliable leap of faith.

In 1986, Howard opened Il Giornale, Italian for The Daily, in Seattle. It was an immediate success with 300 customers coming in on its first day alone. He was already thinking of expanding.

A year later the original Starbucks was looking to sell.

He knew this was an opportunity he couldn't pass up. So he went right to his creditors, explaining his vision for a community atmosphere centered on the experience of drinking coffee. All he needed was quality beans and the infrastructure to move forward. They could sense the passion in Schultz and he had a proven track record of being a successful investment. The investors were ready to see the next phase of Schultz's plan come to fruition: a coffee shop on every corner. With their support, his final step was set in motion.

Success would continue to follow Howard Schultz in making his vision a reality.

In 2000, he stepped down as CEO of the company; however, after eight years he returned, as the company had lost its focus. Schultz reminded those at Starbucks that "we're not in the business of filling bellies; we're in the business of filling souls."

After doing some re-branding and closing of stores, Schultz turned the coffee empire around. Today, Starbucks continues to lead all companies in selling coffee drinks to people all over the world. In June 2018, Howard decided to step down again and step away from the dominant coffee company he had created. At the time of his voluntary leave, Starbucks had grown to 28,000 stores in 77 countries with around three million people employed by Schultz over the decades. He had certainly made his dreams a reality.

Takeaway

How did Schultz build such a reliable company brand? He followed his business principles along with his vision. He not only viewed the customer as a close friend but developed the mindset of "treat people like family and they will be loyal and give their all."

Fads come and go, and people often chase after them. But what would happen if a business kept trying to follow every fad?

It would risk losing a customer base that had come to expect a certain experience when walking into a store. Imagine Starbucks trying to enlist Crocs, fidget spinners, and the hot new app into their store experience. It would seem frivolous. Walking up to the counter at a Starbucks, you expect the green hat with the Starbucks symbol on the employee who takes your order. You know you have to remember whether a Venti is a small or a medium. And, you wait to see if they spelled your name right on the cup when your drink arrives. You can expect the same experience at every Starbucks. They have created a foundational business model that customers can expect no matter where they are in the world.

Starbucks offers customers a consistent cup of coffee and an inviting environment for work or leisure. They make it a point to know their customers!

Schultz's company and mindset can be summed up with this:

> "I think our responsibility as entrepreneurs is not only to build a great business and to dream big, but also to recognize our responsibility to pay it forward to other people.… And I think it's fair to say that the rules of engagement and personal responsibility for every business person and every business leader are much different today than ever before. We can't rely on and wait for government to solve all our problems. It's our responsibility to give back to our communities and to bring our people along with us on the journey."

Schultz found success by first finding a passion for transforming the way we view a product. He then took that vision and planned out actionable steps for making that vision a reality. Along the way, he made sure to create a brand around the value of treating the people around him like family. But he made sure to keep himself looking forward to his vision and values. Beyond this, be ready for your light-bulb moment when it arrives.

Fun Facts

- Starbucks currently employs around 360,000 people.
- Howard was turned down 217 of the 242 times he approached people for investments in the early days of his company.

There's nothing more pathetic than a man who devotes all the hours of the day to the making of money for money's sake.
You must have a larger ambition.

John
ROCKEFELLER

Despite having to bear heavy responsibilities at a young age, John learned lessons of self-control, focus, and work ethic that he later applied in life to show the world what can be accomplished with purpose, vision, planning, and execution.

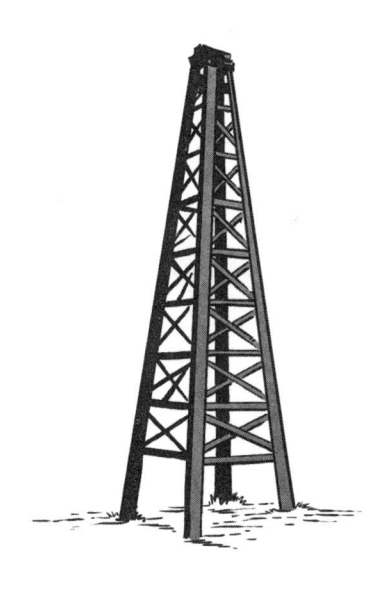

"The man who starts out simply with the idea of getting rich won't succeed; you must have a larger ambition."

The Oil Titan

When we think of someone living the American dream, we think of a self-made person who rose from rags to riches. Accomplishing this dream takes hard work, determination, and problem-solving skills. In this chapter, we will look to someone who embodied all of these traits, a man who made a template for how to become rich: John D Rockefeller.

Rockefeller was arguably the most important industrialist of his time, and undoubtedly one of the most influential entrepreneurial-minded investors ever. We will examine this man who held to certain core beliefs throughout his life, ones that can lead to success in the world of finance and life itself.

Rags to Riches

John Davison Rockefeller was born in 1839 in Richford, New York. His parents were William "Bill" Avery Rockefeller and Eliza Davison Rockefeller. His mother played a major role in his character development, as she was a very religious woman. This religious upbringing shaped his attitude to the importance of "get money and give money" that he would follow throughout his life.

However, Rockefeller's father was essentially a snake oil salesman who was often on the road. He was an unreliable father figure throughout Rockefeller's upbringing, constantly coming in and out of his life. This made the young Rockefeller mature quickly as he took on responsibilities around the house. This meant his childhood was short-lived. He soon became the father figure to his other siblings and learned the importance of hard work, leadership, and caring for others at a young age.

Through his mother and mentors at his local church, he was taught the value of self-improvement and maintaining honor for himself and his community—a set of ideals he would later take with him into the business world.

His mother taught him "control of self wins the battle, for it means control of others."

Rockefeller did not excel in school because of his extra responsibilities at home. The traditional school system considered him slow, untalented, and below average in his studies. Although he struggled, he was never known as being a slacker. Even from a young age, people remembered Rockefeller for working hard and being focused, quiet, and reserved. Teachers respected John's ability to control his emotions and desires, and to focus on his work. He was always looking to point his efforts towards the aims he had envisioned. He was a young boy who understood that he might not be naturally gifted in the traditional sense but was willing to work harder than the person next to him. That's one of the hardest first steps towards success.

Even during his younger years, he had a fire burning inside of him—a desire for more. Young Rockefeller did have one traditionally academic skill he excelled at: arithmetic. He enjoyed the game of numbers, but everything else in school became burdensome, and he started feeling as though traditional education was holding him back. This led him to him dropping out to enroll in a business course where he learned bookkeeping, penmanship, and banking.

He was able to graduate at the age of 16, ready to enter the workforce. He figured out what he wanted out of life and went for it!

With his ability to maintain a clear mind, free from emotion, he was well equipped for making decisions in the business world. He followed the principle that the only way to be your own boss is to be able to boss yourself around.

To escape his small-town Ohio home, Rockefeller moved to Cleveland. Upon arriving, he was ready to get to work and continue learning and developing his business skills. He understood that he needed to sell himself as a hard worker to get his foot in the door. He created a list of all the top financial institutions in the city and went door to door expressing his understanding of business and bookkeeping, willingness to learn, and, maybe most importantly, his ambitious attitude.

As with most success stories, he was not immediately successful in this door-to-door job search, but he persisted. He went through his entire list, and no job offers materialized, so he started at the top and went through again. Failure was not an option.

Rockefeller had made an important realization: no matter the job, no matter what he was doing toward his goals, the business was him. In this case, he was looking for work. Thus, he was in the business of looking for work. Every day, he worked at his business. This mindset would prove essential for his long-term success and motivated him to keep learning so he could maintain an edge on everyone else.

Lessons in the Rise

Rockefeller's persistence would pay off. On September 26, 1855, he was given a chance by a small produce firm, Hewitt & Tuttle, as an assistant bookkeeper.

Although the title was not flashy, this was an important moment in Rockefeller's life. It was his first big break. It was his opportunity to get his foot in the door of business and would propel him into the corporate giant that he eventually became.

In the world of business, we too often think of the business leader on Wall Street with the loud, expressive, and assertive demeanor. This type of person has their positive traits, but Rockefeller took a different approach; he was much quieter and reserved, looking to consume information while keeping his inner thoughts to himself. This allowed him to maintain a clear mind when he needed to make important decisions. While some leaders become flustered, nervous, and agitated during high-pressure moments, Rockefeller made it a point to keep his composure to allow him to make clear and deliberate decisions. When others became flustered, Rockefeller remained calm.

John saw strength in silence. "Success comes from keeping the ears open and the mouth closed," he once said.

As Rockefeller worked his way up in the business world, he saw examples of increased power and wealth leading many to dangerous levels of arrogance. He realized this could blind you to your faults, which we all have. He knew he must keep his ego in check in order to maintain a clear mind to continue making wise decisions, otherwise it would lead to his downfall. You don't want all of your hard work to come crumbling down because of simple arrogance!

Rockefeller often engaged in self-reflection. Analyzing his inner thoughts, motivations, and emotions helped him maintain a clear mind, because he was able to learn more about himself and the way he thought. It made it possible to understand his own reasoning, keep his thoughts clear, and avoid becoming infatuated with fame and fortune.

Rockefeller always wanted to stay grounded. Even as his riches started pouring into his bank account, he maintained a connection with his community. He continued attending church, often attending mass multiple times per week. It became a means of meditation for him, a way to clear his mind and maintain foresight for his daily intentions. Before he became wealthy, he could be found sweeping the church halls, ushering people to their seats, studying the bible, praying, singing, and performing various church duties for his congregation. Where many during the time period would frequently upgrade to "higher class" churches, Rockefeller continued to attend the community church of his early years. He enjoyed the connections he made and never wanted to forget where he came from. More importantly, he never forgot the people who helped build him into the man he was becoming.

Many choices that he made helped him remain humble. He made it a point to not allow his ego to get in the way of his decision making. This included asking that various charity projects he funded not include his name.

The Oil Man

The oil refinery boom swept the nation in the early 1860s. America was hooked; they had found an abundant form of energy! Luckily for Rockefeller, Cleveland was around 100 miles from the major oil region of the time. He was ready to see what the fuss was all about.

Rockefeller was a calculated and organized man, and the early days of the oil boom were everything but organized! Oil mining accidents, oil flooded rivers, and inefficient gathering of oil was rampant. Additionally, the early oil market had major price fluctuations that appalled him.

Even with all the red flags coming from the oil market, Rockefeller saw opportunity. His first goal was to cut wastefulness: where others would throw out excess from the oil making process, Rockefeller went looking for uses. He sold the gasoline that was produced as fuel, while others dumped it in rivers. John found a use for the tar by selling it for paving, and his team discovered the oil byproducts for lubricants, oil, and candles. Where others were throwing away these products, John was profiting.

By 1870 he had formed Standard Oil. Rockefeller had become the most efficient oil producer, while also maintaining the highest quality product. As his profits increased, he invested in projects to find more efficient production measures and even more by-products. You could say the business was a well-oiled machine!

John had turned a product the rich primarily used into a product for all.

Takeaway

In the end, John D. Rockefeller became the most dominant business force in history. He made sure he kept his ego in check, kept his emotions at bay, and followed his principles. This made him the ultimate decision maker. Once he formed his efficient and high-quality oil company, the next step was continued expansion. Others did not catch on to his system, and Rockefeller either bought up or gave shares to other oil companies. After buying, he would implement his methods to make the company his own.

But after all of this success, he maintained his roots. He maintained that his best decisions were marrying his wife and accepting Jesus as his Savior. He made sure to pray, go to church, and keep himself connected to the community. His connection with God led him to the desire to give back. He attacked his charitable work as a business, looking to find more efficient means and innovation. If a university he donated to found success in their research, he would donate more!

His method: give to those eager to produce, serve, and improve. And in the end, he looked to be a beacon of the principles he held true—clear your mind, serve, make the world better, and give back. He mastered who he was.

Go out and find who you are, live who you are, and follow who you are because nobody else will.

Fun Facts

- Rockefeller's goal was to reach the age of 100. He almost made it but died at the age of 97!

- In retirement John found solace in his love for plants and flowers.

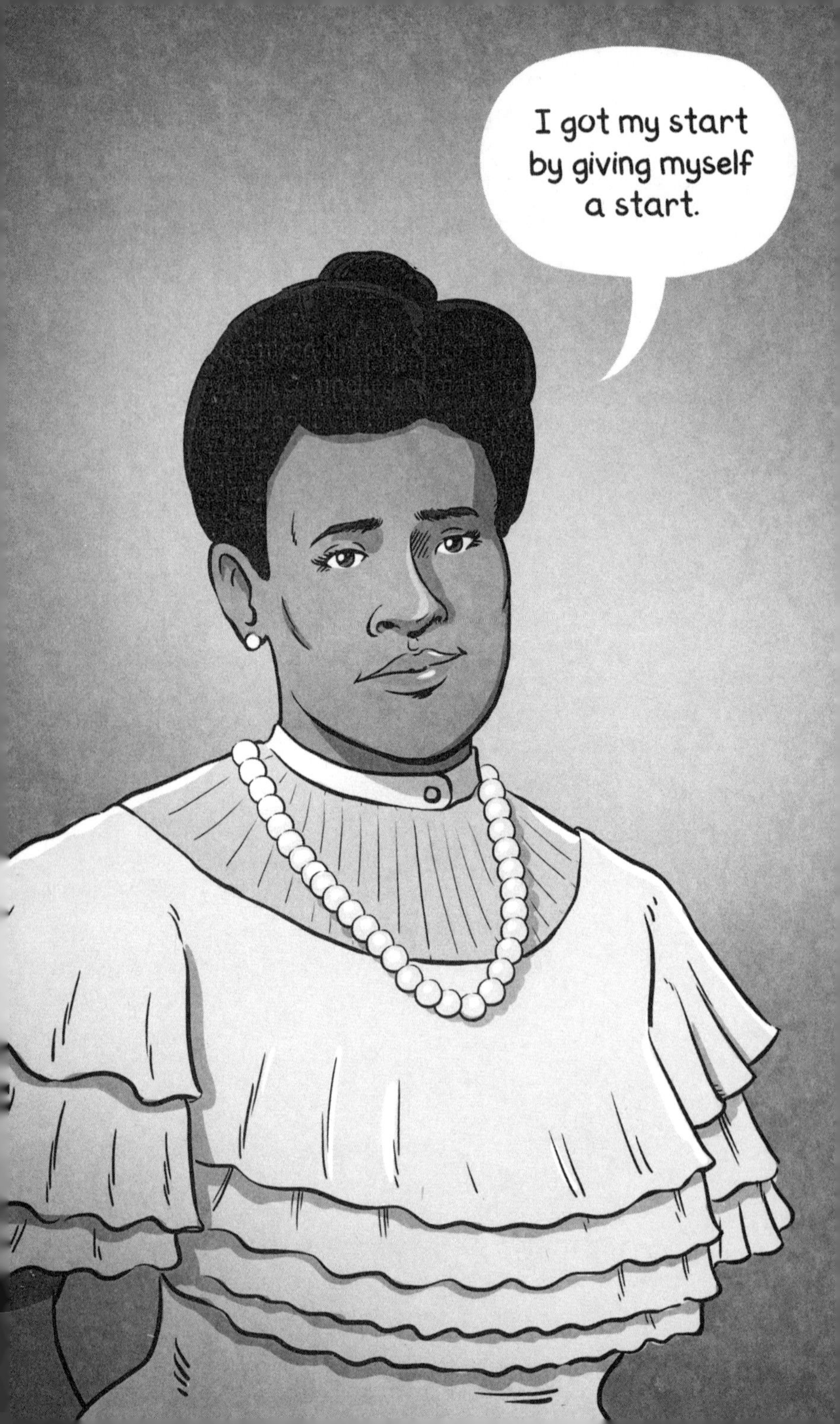
I got my start by giving myself a start.

Madam
WALKER

After overcoming significant oppression to become the first black millionaire, Madam Walker felt compelled to use her wealth and knowledge to empower other women and fight against the extreme racism that was ravaging post-slavery America.

"I am in the business world, not for myself alone… but to do all the good I can for the uplifting of my race."

The Self-Made Woman

There is a commonly held belief that minorities and women in the workforce need to be protected by the government from prejudice and discrimination. But is this reality? This image seems to ignore the various economic trends that have shown steady improvements in the number of women and minority leaders in business, improved pay, and increased opportunities, all due to the effects of private enterprise.

One woman in particular, Madam C. J. Walker, took advantage of the opportunities that existed in a free enterprise system. She was a black woman who was born just after the time slavery was abolished in the U.S.

It was a fascinating time. The end of slavery sparked a vast migration of African-Americans across the country. These formerly enslaved people now had the freedom to take part in the free market. Walker's story helped change the narrative about the abilities of both women and black people in America, where people were beginning to understand every human had the capacity to be a successful entrepreneur.

"It is reliably claimed," her biographer John Blundell once wrote, that "she was the first woman ever to make a million without an inheritance, husband or government intervention. She did it on her own."

Upbringing

Madam Walker, as she was later known, was born Sarah Breedlove on December 23, 1867, to former slaves of a

Louisiana cotton plantation. She was the first free child born in the family. She faced many obstacles early in her life. The first was her parents' deaths in a yellow fever epidemic that hit the area. This forced her to live with her older sister. Unfortunately, her sister's husband was cruel, which likely motivated Sarah to leave the household at the age of fourteen to marry Moses McWilliams. He died seven years later, leaving her alone with their three-year-old daughter Lelia. Fortunately, she kept moving forward even with the many heartbreaking obstacles she had already faced.

Sarah was ready to make the best of her situation. She and her daughter packed up their things and moved to St. Louis, where three of her brothers resided. She found work as a washerwoman and remarried in 1894. Although things were starting to look up for her, tragedy struck again. Sarah's husband had a drinking problem and was unfaithful. She found herself financially supporting his poor life decisions.

It was time for a change. Creating a stable life for her daughter was her top priority. She had a vision of a better life.

The Problem

During this racially charged time, Sarah had to overcome even more obstacles than most. She had to overcome the limits set by society that halted the progress of many women and minorities.

But she saw a problem that needed solving and knew she had a solution. During her time, black women often experienced baldness from scalp disease, often caused by harmful hair products, poor diet, and stress.

She earned an opportunity as a sales agent for Annie Turnbo Pope Malone's Poro Co, selling the "wonderful hair grower" This is when she saw an opportunity. Sarah struggled with hair loss herself and recognized something other entrepreneurs didn't during the time: the economic potential of marketing to black women.

She took her daughter and one dollar and fifty cents to Denver, Colorado. There, she found her third husband, Charles Joseph Walker, a skilled newspaper salesman. With him, she was able to establish a hair care business.

Sarah, now Madam Walker, designed a unique hair care product, inspired by the company she'd worked for previously, and started testing it on herself. Soon, her hair began regrowing! Her marketing strategy was to place ads for the hair care products in the newspapers aimed at black readers, a market that was quickly growing. An entrepreneur was born.

Walker's success was not just the result of offering an effective product. Her true genius was recognizing that a segment of the market was being ignored. Other hair product companies were marketing only to white people as potential customers because that was their original market. They hadn't realized the potential of directing their marketing to the African Americans who were rising along the economic ladder after being freed from slavery.

Marketing her hair care product in newspapers written for black audiences worked like a charm. Her hair care products found their way into almost every black home across

America. She also had a charismatic style that led her to have a loyal customer base. She not only had a fantastic product, but she was also willing to use her personality to propel it further.

Business Details

In 1910, she moved her business to Indianapolis, Indiana, and created Madam C. J. Walker Hair Culturists Union of America.

Walker revolutionized what it meant to market your product. Her dedication and hard work made her name and image well known to both black and white women all across the country. Part of her business plan was to give lectures and demonstrations on how to properly use marketing to sell her products. Her method was to invite people from across the country to her various beauty schools to be trained on her products and the sale of them. She would get them to buy into the company culture. Once training was complete, the sales agents would set out door to door with the product or set up their own physical shops. This training empowered her salespeople to sell with confidence. Walker's kind, outgoing, and caring personality inspired passionate loyalty from her community of 40,000 female employees.

This was a time when women were not even allowed to vote. Walker was able to subvert the oppressive barbarism of the government by empowering women in her own way; she employed them to the point that they could attain economic freedom. They looked up to a woman who faced down the prejudices of the time and succeeded despite them. Walker inspired people because she stopped looking to others to create the life she wanted to live.

To put all of this into perspective: during this time of racial segregation, where unskilled, white, male workers were earning an average of $11 a week, her black, female sales agents were making $5 to $15 a day.

Later Work

After much success with her business, she became a leading philanthropist for the black community. She built a YMCA in Indianapolis and restored Frederick Douglass's home. She continued her community involvement by participating in the protest movement taking place across the country against lynching.

Walker recognized the obstacles she had to overcome in her life and felt compelled to make her voice heard against the social and political racism that was still apparent across America. Although money was important for her to be able to provide a comfortable life and schooling for her daughter, it was not her end goal. Money allowed her to become the active philanthropist she desired to be.

Takeaway

Walker's passion for her product, ability to overcome obstacles, and care for the black community continues to inspire people many years after her death. Throughout her life, she made sure to emphasize the importance of the entrepreneurial mindset and the power of working hard in a free market society. She used her success in the free market to spread her wealth to others, whether it was through her philanthropy, or simply teaching others the skills she had learned from her successes and failures in the world of business. In the end, she has gone down in history as an example of the empowerment all people can experience through free enterprise.

"More than any other single businessperson," a Harvard professor later remarked, "Walker unveiled the vast economic potential of an African-American economy, even one stifled and suffocating under Jim Crow segregation."

Fun Facts

- Madam C. J. Walker called her premium hair treatment the "Wonderful Hair Grower."

- The women she trained were nicknamed the "beauty evangelists."

There are countless opportunities to take shortcuts, but I would destroy my mission in life if I took those shortcuts.

Magatte WADE

Why hasn't Africa experienced more wealth despite having received so much international aid from other countries? Magatte Wade knows that corrupt governments and heavy regulations are what is stopping business growth—and she is showing others why entrepreneurship is so critical to help those in need.

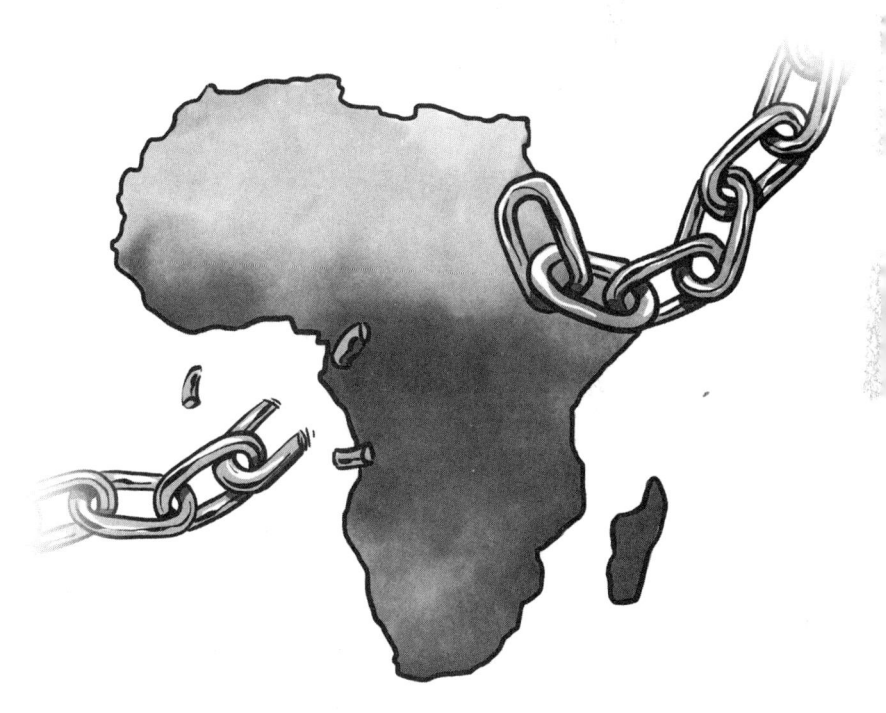

"It takes next to nothing to start."

A Love of Freedom

In the previous chapters, we've covered the economic movers and shakers here in the United States, but we need to remember that free enterprise occurs around the world. Magatte Wade is a creative mind looking to spread the idea of free enterprise to the people of Africa.

Magatte has become one of the leading entrepreneurs in Africa.

But this entrepreneur is a little different from the rest. Her entrepreneurial challenges and realizations have made her a strong voice in defending the creative power of free markets. Wade's entrepreneurial fortitude and prowess have made her an important figure in spreading the concept of free markets on the international stage.

The Free Spirit

Wade spent the first few years of her life with her family in Senegal, where the majority of the population works in agriculture with a depressed economy.

Her parents left for Europe searching for work, and she was raised by her grandparents. They allowed her to independently explore and go on adventures. She developed a curious mind for everything around her. She often wondered why things are the way they are.

When she turned eight, her parents wanted to ensure she received a proper education. Unfortunately, in Senegal, skipping school was a common occurrence. So her parents decided it was time she moved to Germany with them to attend school there. Germany was a turning point for her. Along with her first encounters with snow, she noticed the prosperous economy, developed streets, and city luxuries.

After a couple of years, her family moved to France for work. Her high school in France had an exchange program that provided the opportunity for her to live in America. She attended a university in Indiana that would become an important experience in her life. Her time in the exchange program allowed her to make connections that helped her to pursue other opportunities.

There was something about America that she could not shake: the entrepreneurial spirit. This spirit is one that fit like a piece to her own puzzle, one that she attributed to being a free spirit like her mother.

When she went back to her hometown in Senegal, she noticed major differences between it and America. The two countries were like night and day. This made her wonder, why does one country produce an innovative, developed society, and the other get left behind?

Connecting her ideas later in life, she realized that a couple of decades ago, China was in the same boat as many African countries, but today they are arguably the greatest economic nation in the world. This left Wade wondering why places like Singapore, Hong Kong, and even Dubai (surrounded by sand) made it, but places like Senegal fell by the wayside. These countries have very different cultures, geography, and resources but all were able to accomplish similar prosperity. What did they do differently?

She realized it had nothing to do with the people and

their choices, but something else entirely. In each of those thriving countries, people had the freedom to express themselves and create as they desired. That is what built the road to prosperity.

Personal Responsibility

Wade went on to start her own company in 2004. She started Adina after returning to Senegal and being disappointed that corporate drinks like Coke and Fanta had begun to outsell Bissap, a traditional beverage made from ingredients found in Senegal. Instead of looking to the government for answers and creating restrictions against foreign-owned soft drink companies, she innovated! She had a desire, located a need, and believed her idea would create value—so she went after it.

She realized the only way to protect her cultural traditions was to show the West what her culture is about. In the process, the Senegalese people would also take pride in respecting their own traditions. She took matters into her own hands from a feeling of personal responsibility.

Luckily for Wade, she started her company around the time Whole Foods was spreading across the United States. People not only wanted more nature-inspired products, but they wanted to explore alternative beverage and food options from other cultures. Magatte's drink company was a perfect fit! By 2010 the annual revenues of Adina had exceeded $3.5 million. Magatte Wade has a knack for business!

After starting the company, it took her only five years to raise a whopping $30 million in funding. However, this massive capital expansion had its drawbacks. With more money coming in from other parties with interests of their own, the company stopped feeling like her project. She missed the freedom to style her brand and the products she wanted to create.

Wade no longer felt her beliefs were being expressed in the business. It had moved away from her vision. A new vision needed to be made!

She stepped down as Adina's CEO in 2009, though she still holds a stake in the company.

Even though she stepped down, this wasn't the end of Wade's vision. She had another plan at the ready! As most successful entrepreneurs understand, when one business venture closes, it creates another door of opportunity ready to be opened.

Wade opened that door by founding Tiossan and Skin is Skin. Both of these companies are trying to bring jobs and economic opportunities to the people of Senegal. For Skin is Skin, Wade has created a natural product that uses local products, creating jobs in her country.

Unfortunately, Senegal ranks 124 out of 159 on the Fraser Institute's economic freedom ranking. A ranking that low comes with a lot of implications for the business owners in Senegal. Wade is looking to change that by showing the Senegalese people the economic opportunities provided by less government control and regulation.

The poor regulatory policies of Senegal has shown Wade the dangers of overregulation. She knew Senegal was not the best environment for starting a business, but her vision is to help her home country learn, grow, and understand economic prosperity.

One of the issues she faced is she couldn't get all the products she needed from her country. She needed to import some. However, Senegal wanted to charge her a 45% tariff for it! Imagine finding an amazing product from another country with a set price, but you go to checkout online only to find you must pay a government-mandated fee of almost half the price. Does that sound fair?

To get around this mandated fee, Wade had to go through mountains of paperwork. These disadvantages like high tariffs not only deter people in Senegal from going after their creative desires and visions, but those who want to pursue a business idea often take it elsewhere, which means Senegal has fewer jobs available to people who want to work. If people are not able to be employed, not only does the economy struggle, but the individuals in that country struggle. No businesses, no jobs, no income means the people are poor, and worse yet, the people are suffering. The overregulation from the Senegalese government is detrimental to the development of the country.

You see, the problem facing places with overregulation like Senegal isn't that people don't want to work, it's that there are no jobs for them to work. "We need to streamline the business environment for Africa to become prosperous," she has said—making clear that these barriers and hurdles create problems for people who want to become entrepreneurs and create millions of middle class jobs to lift poor people into prosperity.

Takeaway

Even with the recent divergence from the principles of free enterprise, America is still seen as the land of opportunity throughout the world. This narrative is not so much the case for many countries in Africa, causing many to have a negative perception of doing business there.

Something Magatte Wade found is that people are more willing to donate to a charity than to buy from African businesses. As the saying goes, it's better to teach people to fish instead of giving them a fish. Yet, people are more than happy to donate to a non-profit handing out fish. But who is helping the people learn how to fish?

For example, Tom's Shoes has a "buy a shoe, give a shoe" campaign where the company will donate a pair of shoes in the developing world for every pair it sells. Well, it turns out that actually hurts businesses in Africa. It's hard for African shoe-making businesses to compete with free shoes. This forces them to close and jobs to disappear. Good intentions don't always lead to good outcomes. Someone needs to remind the government of this lesson!

A lesson Wade learned from her first business, Adina, was that people involved with her business need to hold a similar vision. Everyone from the partners, investors, employees, and stakeholders need to not only understand the vision of the company but share in the purpose that is being worked toward. Otherwise, your business will be in danger of transforming into something else entirely.

She also recognized the importance of selling in business. If you lack the skills to sell your product, then you need to find a partner who can. Sometimes we need to be honest with ourselves and be willing to seek help in areas that we're lacking. Without the ability to sell, you will never be able to spread the vision you have to the world.

But maybe the most important lesson to take from Magatte Wade is that as we come to understand that the free market thrives with the human desire for personal responsibility, we need to spread that message to others. That's exactly what Wade is looking to do.

Fun Facts

- "Adina" means "life" in her native language, Wolof.
- In 2011, she was named a Young Global Leader at the World Economic Forum

At age twelve, I had already set my mind on a great industrial career in the new mechanical age.

Powel
CROSLEY

New technologies ignited the imagination of a Cincinnati teenager whose life's work and innovative contributions have significantly shaped much of our modern culture and way of life.

"I decided it was about time for me to take a swing at the world."

The Innovative Entrepreneur

Powel Crosley once bragged that he never made over 50 dollars a week before the age of 30. While most people wouldn't boast about something so embarrassing, most people aren't Powel Crosley. However, by the time he hit thirty, Crosley was one of the most famous business magnates of the early 20th century.

That's not to say the man achieved success in everything he tried. A college dropout, Crosley's love of automobiles, at a time when cars were still new technology, drove him in his future endeavors, for better or worse. While the name Crosley is still well-known among classic car enthusiasts, it was his pioneering work in the radio industry that made him a household name.

We don't see the name Powel Crosley written in many places nowadays. The Crosley Broadcasting Corporation, Crosley Automobiles, and Crosley Stadium are all remnants of an older, simpler era. He may not be as well-known today as Henry Ford, but Crosley's innovative achievements in the automotive, radio, military, and sports industries are some of the most important in history.

Crosley The Car Boy

Born in Cincinnati in 1886, Powel Crosley grew up right alongside the modern automobile. Mechanics were his passion from childhood, and at age 13, he even attempted to build a car himself. When his father bet him $10 the car couldn't drive the distance of a single block, Crosley created his own electric motor with his brother's help. The car worked. Powel Crosley got his ten dollars from his dad and began a lifetime obsession with the automotive world.

While car manufacturing companies were widespread in the early twentieth century, Crosley didn't have much success starting his own. He learned the mass production techniques popularized by Henry Ford and secured investment for a prototype he called the Marathon Six, a six-cylinder vehicle that would retail for about $1,700—a low-end luxury price. Crosley's engineering know-how couldn't overcome the economic woes of the time. A financial panic scared investors and dried up his funding. Crosley shut down the Marathon Six Automotive company before it sold a single car.

Undeterred, Crosley continued to pursue work in the automotive industry. He wrote advertisements for automotive trade journals, sold cars for manufacturers, and even volunteered as part of a racing team. Yet his dream of starting his own automotive production company continued to elude him.

Crosley's first fortune came from selling automotive parts rather than the cars themselves. He was a genius when it came to innovating new parts, including a tire liner that would later become his best-seller. In 1916, he founded the American Automobile Accessory Company, and by 1919, sales reached one million dollars in a single year.

Crosley understood how to reach and maintain business success. While he focused on developing products, his brother Lewis handled the financial side of the company, ensuring that each brother could focus on what they did best. Crosley was also one of the first to offer a money-back guarantee, which created trust between his company and the buyers. This is a marketing technique that is still widely used today! Much of what Crosley and his brother accomplished is standard today. At the time, they were innovators in American industry of the highest sort.

However, he wasn't a well-known figure across the country. Auto vendors loved his straightforward business style and amazing products, but ordinary Americans learned the Powel Crosley name from the early twentieth century's other great invention: the radio.

The Crosley Broadcasting Company

By 1921 Powel Crosley was a business owner and family man, with a young son who also maintained an interest in new technology. Crosley's son—Powel Crosley III—desperately wanted a radio, a new technology at the time. The elder Crosley balked at the expense and decided to help his son build his own radio.

Crosley discovered a hidden passion for radio technology. He said:

> I read the book and it intrigued me. A couple of days later I went back to the shop and asked if I could buy the parts separately and assemble the radio myself. For between $20 and $25 I returned home with headphones, a tuning coil, a crystal detector, a condenser, and other mystifying gadgets.
>
> Before I knew it, I had virtually forgotten my regular business in the interest of radio. I wondered how other men on salaries as small as mine managed to buy radio

sets at the prices advertised. I knew that the expensive equipment I had been shown was out of the question for them. I also knew that many men lacked the mechanical knowledge—or desire—to build their own sets. I was confident that the radio set was not going to be a rich man's toy and that it had to be within the reach of everyone.

An innovative mind with an entrepreneurial interest was fast at work.

In time, with the help of engineering students from the University of Cincinnati, Crosley was able to manufacture a crystal radio that cost only $7. He named it the Harko and put it up for sale in 1921. By 1925, the Crosley Radio Corporation was the world's largest radio manufacturer.

As with his earlier automotive venture, Crosley designed new products that listeners adored. He developed the first car radio in 1930—the "Roamio." Drivers in Cincinnati could listen to Crosley's radio station, WLW, which was the first to broadcast at 50 watts (high end for the time). WLW—popularly known as "The Nation's Station"—broadcast some of the earliest soap operas, along with acts from performers who would later become world famous, such as Red Skelton and Rosemary Clooney. His station's signal was so powerful it could be heard in Europe and South America.

Crosley had found a way to spread his name far and wide.

The Business Magnate

Most entrepreneurial tales of the 1920s end in the 30s, when the Great Depression harmed or destroyed even successful companies. Crosley didn't just maintain his businesses at this time; the 1930s were some of his brightest years.

A huge part of his success came from his diversification. Crosley manufactured various other home appliances apart from radio sets, which still sold well throughout the dark times of the Great Depression. He manufactured an early refrigerator called the Icyball, which needed no electricity to run. In 1932, Crosley created the first refrigerator with shelves—the "Shelvador." The product's name is obscure, but the innovation is standard today.

Some Crosley products remain obscure novelties, even though they sold well at the time. His Cervac system promised to cure male baldness. It obviously didn't work, but Crosley—who was bald—had one of his own. It's still in his bedroom at his Pinecroft estate, which is now a popular wedding venue. He also owned another product his company developed—the autogym, which promised weight loss and better health with no effort at all.

These products may seem silly to us now, and they probably did back then, too. Crosley's business success, however, was completely serious. His radio and automotive companies continued to expand, helping the government in the war effort by broadcasting "Voice of America" programs and developing experimental vehicles and other military products. Crosley's company even developed the proximity fuze, considered one of the most important technological advancements in WWII.

Crosley himself had nothing to do with the fuze, however. He had no military clearance and couldn't even enter the area of his plant where they were manufactured. General Patton claimed that without the fuze, which Crosley's company manufactured, America would never have won the Battle of the Bulge.

Crosley's companies had weathered the Depression and helped defeat the Axis powers. At the war's end, there was no sign that Crosley would face any adversity in his next venture.

It was time to return to his first love: making his own automobiles. With everything Powel Crosley had learned, built, and accomplished, Crosley Motors Incorporated was poised to stand alongside Ford and Chrysler.

It wasn't to be.

Crosley's Unfulfilled Dream

The first car bearing the name Crosley debuted in 1939, but automobile production ceased during WWII. Immediately after the war's end in 1945, Crosley was ready to put all of his entrepreneurial efforts into making cars that would bear his name. His childhood passion remained as strong as ever.

What had changed, however, was the fuel economy. With rationing over and the economy growing, Americans had started preferring larger cars that needed more fuel. Crosley manufactured compact cars that, while boasting excellent mileage, didn't catch on with the public. Sales declined year over year after WWII until Crosley Motors had to close shop in 1952.

That's not to say Crosley lacked innovation in this field. He was the first to put disc brakes in all of his cars, and the first to introduce push-button starters. He even created the term "Sport Utility Vehicle," among other innovations. Crosley's vehicles are mainstays of the classic car circuit and were solid, elegant vehicles that simply never took off with the public.

Crosley's place in the Automotive Hall of Fame is well-deserved. Still, the importance of consumer preference outweighs any entrepreneurial insight, no matter how ingenious.

America's Pastime

Crosley remained wealthy throughout the Great Depression while many of his friends and colleagues lost huge sums of money. When a man named Sidney Weil lost most of his wealth in the 1929 crash, he sold off one of his main assets: the Cincinnati Reds. Powel Crosley became the proud owner of one of America's most popular yet cash-strapped baseball teams.

Always a keen innovator, Crosley saw the potential in combining radio and baseball, a relationship which continues to this day. He made sure every game got a play-by-play broadcast on his WLW radio station and installed electric stadium lights at what was then named Crosley Stadium. There, supporters watched the first night game in baseball history, while fans throughout the nation listened along on Crosley radios.

He became the innovator that brought baseball to all ears.

Crosley could even be credited for making baseball America's pastime!

Crosley wasn't a particularly die-hard fan of baseball, but he did make sure his team got all the support it deserved. With night game attendance far greater than day games, the Reds' financial situation greatly improved. Radio broadcasts of games were so popular that every team offered them by the late 1930s. Having the stadium named after him wasn't simply an act of ego, without Crosley, the team would have been shuttered. Instead, the Reds remain one of baseball's most historically popular teams.

America's Forgotten Entrepreneur

The Cincinnati Reds no longer play in Crosley Stadium. After his death in 1969, the team moved to Riverside Stadium. By that time Crosley had already sold his main corporation to a different company, which renamed it after he passed. With Crosley Motors and Crosley radios defunct, the once-legendary Crosley name was lost to history.

Crosley lives on in the numerous estates and wildlife preserves he left to charity. While there are products today that still bear the Crosley name, they have little to no connection to Crosley's original companies. The dozens of new inventions and ideas Crosley released are his true legacy.

The man didn't set out to make sure his name would last for an eternity. Crosley was not an iconoclast or an egotist. He was an entrepreneur, through and through, the kind who understands innovation, success, and hard work are their own reward.

In that sense, Crosley is among the greatest inventors America has ever seen. Any time you switch on a radio, push-button start a car, or even put something on a refrigerator shelf, remember that it's Crosley who helped make that happen.

Fun Facts

- He is nicknamed "The Henry Ford of radios."
- By 1925 Crosley Radio corporation was producing 5,000 radios a day—the largest radio manufacturer in the world.

Going to bed at night saying "we've done something wonderful"... That's what matters to me.

Steve
JOBS

Raised in an area where computer technologies were first beginning to develop, Steve saw that a future once only depicted in science fiction was actually possible. What he didn't yet see was that he was going to be the one to help make it a reality.

"Most people never pick up the phone and call. Most people never ask. And that's what separates, sometimes, the people that do things from the people that just dream about them. You gotta act and you gotta be willing to fail."

The Marketing Guru

The world will never forget the role Steve Jobs played in creating the digital age, from the impact of his computers to the innovation of the smartphone.

He was known for being a perfectionist almost to a fault. His perfectionist personality was extended into how he treated people in relationships. He expected everything to run perfectly. If things went south, he would become temperamental and difficult to get along with.

So why focus on an innovative figure who had so many faults? Well, there are lessons to be learned from those with minds for innovation and insights to be learned from their shortcomings. Sometime those faults are the very traits that lead to their success.

Jobs is often characterized as an opportunist who worked off the backs of others by making other people's inventions prettier. But he recognized some of his shortcomings, allowing him to focus on what he did well. It's one thing to be innovative and create something foundational, but it's important to remember marketing and presentation. And Steve Jobs was a once-in-a-generation artist for his ability to do just that.

He provides a lesson in how entrepreneurial traits can drive you to greatness, but also serves as a caution that you must watch the effects those traits have in all areas of life.

Upbringing

Steve Jobs was adopted as a baby by Paul and Clara Jobs. This helped shape his innovative mind, as his adoptive parents lived in Santa Clara County—known today as Silicon Valley.

These were the early years of Silicon Valley, but some early tech companies were already taking the area over. Jobs grew up around neighbors who were engineers and constantly had gadgets, electronics, and gizmos to work with. A perfect formula for sparking the interest of a young innovative mind!

Jobs remained fascinated by the technology he grew up around through his teenage years. When it came time for college, he attended Reed College in Oregon. He lasted one semester before he realized his mind was expanding elsewhere.

He had found himself fascinated by other areas such as eastern philosophy and a desire to understand himself and the world around him. Jobs moved to an Oregon commune to begin his explorative journey, which eventually took him to India in 1974. While he was there, he came to fully embrace Buddhist philosophy.

Story

A major part of understanding Steve Jobs is knowing how much he valued eastern philosophy and spirituality. His beliefs were a key factor in how he ran Apple, his company that took the world by storm. They were the way he was able to better understand himself and the vision he wanted for the world. It allowed him to answer the question "how can I bring value to the world?" in his own way.

Author Joseph Campbell sheds light on Steve Jobs' life

through the analogy of the hero's journey. He points out that a common thread through the journey of all hero stories is that they leave what is familiar to claim victory in new surroundings, at which point, they return to share their wisdom. In the case of Steve Jobs, he left his boyhood home in Silicon Valley to live in India and learn about Buddhism before returning to implement those ideas in a business setting back in California.

Jobs already had a tremendous passion for math, science, and electronics: an essential skill set for finding new innovations in the engineering industry. He knew where his expertise and interest were, but he needed a way to channel what he knew into an effective path to create value for others. This is where his eastern philosophy became foundational to helping him maintain the right mindset.

Practicing meditation helped him develop a masterful ability to focus. When facing deadlines and the pressure to execute and succeed, the ability to focus becomes a must. His spiritual mindset allowed him to put an idea into his mind that he wanted to go after, and then do everything in his power to make it happen.

This became his master tool in the art of the entrepreneur's mindset.

What makes Steve Jobs' story so interesting and inspiring? Well, let's get back to his hero's journey. Often in the hero's journey we think the character needs to overcome some physical obstacle, but in the world today those obstacles are often our own minds. Thoughts telling us we can't do it or it's already been done or I'm too late or this isn't good enough. These are excuses. In Jobs' journey, he overcame these mental obstacles that were preventing him from making his visions a reality. The vision he discovered was to make technology a human experience, one that we can all share in. Jobs foresaw the potential of this vision decades before anyone else.

Job's journey came when he left his home to move to India to "find himself." He overcame mental obstacles to understand the vision he wanted to give back to the world. He asked himself, "What can I create to help my fellow human?" And like many great inventors, his vision required a keen eye for innovation and an understanding of entrepreneurship. Inventors are the true heroes of our reality, bringing value to us that we never understood we needed.

The vision Steve Jobs foresaw was using technology to build human relationships and connecting the world!

The Man

Upon Steve Jobs's return from India, it wasn't an immediately easy road to success. He met up with his long-time friend Stephen Wozniak (Woz). Woz had a knack for understanding both computer hardware and the software that went into it. This led him to create a personal computer for himself. When Jobs was visiting him one day to check out his hardware, something clicked!

Not everyone had the skill or desire to create a personal computer and then mess with the software. Some just wanted to write code without dealing with the complicated process of building their own computer. This was Steve's light-bulb moment: they could build personal computers for software enthusiasts. Apple Computers was born.

Jobs had many successes with various innovative products including developing personal computers, funding Pixar, and inventing the iPod, iPhone, and iPad. How did his mind allow him to create such innovative products?

Skeptics certainly did their part to try to keep him from succeeding. Their complaints were endless.

"No one needs a computer in their home."

"No one will see a film without live actors."

"Who needs 1000 songs in their pocket?"

"The iPad is just a big iPod touch. Also, it has a stupid name."

But Jobs just kept following his vision of developing innovative products that would improve the lives of his customers.

One of his visions was creating a computer you could use through touch. The consumer did not understand they wanted it—many were skeptical—but he knew they would want it once it existed.

Jobs built his career by creating products that consumers did not understand they wanted. In time, Jobs transformed the skeptics into people proclaiming the products as a necessity. That's innovation!

Part of this innovation was his ability to make established products appear new. In the case of the personal computer, he took an already created product and rebranded it. However, this doesn't mean the product itself wasn't of good quality. This was of utmost importance to Steve—make a great product!

He was more of the mindset that you don't have to be the first to create a new product, but you *must* be the best. Branding and advertising is an art form, though it becomes much easier when you have an amazing product to go with it. Once he had the product designed the way he wanted, he focused on marketing by trying to make the consumer feel a part of something. This came in the form of a clean, sleek, modern look with a reliable product inside of it. Then, he made the Apple experience unique from everything else on the market. Jobs perfected the art of making a product a trend in society!

"When you grow up," Jobs once said, "you tend to get told the world is the way it is and your life is just to live your life inside the world. Try not to bash into the walls too much. Try to have a nice family, have fun, save a little money." He continued: "That's a very limited life. Life can be much broader once you discover one simple fact: Everything around you that you call life was made up by people that were no smarter than you and you can change it, you can influence it, you can build your own things that other people can use. Once you learn that, you'll never be the same again."

His Mindset

Part of understanding Jobs is knowing that he was an unforgiving perfectionist. He expected perfection not only from himself but from those all around him: friends, family, and especially those who worked for him.

After the Apple 2 was released, Jobs' employees were drained and company morale was low. The pressure from Jobs led to high turnover and employees taking less pride in their work. Ultimately, Apple's Board of Directors ended up appointing a corporate babysitter to keep Jobs' temper in check.

When you're thinking about becoming an entrepreneur, you must learn to understand the mindset of your workers. Jobs had skills and limitations of his own! Something he lacked was an understanding of others. Likewise, workers have certain skills and limitations of their own. Although you can point out their faults and wrongdoings, you must appreciate the work they provide when it shows improvement or is of good quality. If you don't, you will face the difficulty that Jobs had to overcome.

Takeaway

Entrepreneurs and innovators know that they're speculators, someone with a willingness to take the risk. But the best entrepreneurial speculators trust the research and have an understanding of their decision-making process so they can fully assess the risks and make choices that have the best possibility for a positive outcome. Entrepreneurs like Steve Jobs only make risky decisions when the decision felt like no risk at all.

However, part of adventuring into the world of entrepreneurship is understanding the unavoidable reality of uncertain events occurring. The best entrepreneurs anticipate these events and predict the desires of the consumer. Steve did this perfectly.

He did this through his creation of innovative and reliable products. But, once these two items were covered, he knew how to convince people to become a part of a community of passionate minds using products to help change the world.

An entrepreneur's success comes from their ability to anticipate future markets, desires, and conditions, and then being organized to capitalize on these potentially profitable predictions. This takes time, effort, fortitude, and adaptability. All traits Jobs had himself. He was a man willing to accept his shortcomings and double down on what he truly believed.

Steve Jobs had an eye for which technological advances would be most fruitful, and he had the marketing eye of no one we've ever seen. Jobs knew what people wanted before they even had the thought that they wanted it. If that's not an entrepreneurial mind, it's hard to know what is.

"Your time is limited," he once said, "so don't waste it living someone else's life."

Fun Facts

- Jobs chose the name Apple after visiting an apple farm.

- He almost became a Buddhist monk after spending time in India.

- He wore a black turtleneck, jeans, and sneakers almost every day.

If you respect your customers as friends, they will support you in good times and bad.

Wally AMOS

Wally's aunt taught him that making cookies in the kitchen can help make friends on the tough streets of Harlem. Little did she know that this life lesson would give Wally the edge in finding friends and fame in the cookie business.

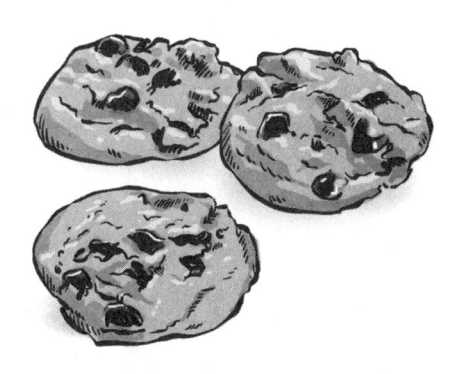

"Being famous is highly overrated."

Sweet Success

When Wally Amos worked as a music industry talent manager, discovering and signing legendary acts like Simon & Garfunkel, Marvin Gaye, and Diana Ross, he had one special advantage no one else could match.

It wasn't just his drive, his intellect, or even the fact that he was the first black talent scout in the nation. What Amos had was sweeter than anything his rivals could offer: chocolate chip cookies.

When Amos sent letters of interest to up-and-coming bands, he would always include a box of sweets he'd baked himself. These delicious treats set him apart from the competition and made a memorable gift to his future clients. Nobody could resist the sweet temptation, and music acts were eager to sign with this memorable manager. He quickly became one of the most successful talent agents in the country.

And he was just getting started.

Wally Amos, better known nowadays as "Famous" Amos, started one of the most well-known cookie companies of the twentieth century. Through all the various ups and downs, including writing ten self-help books and making appearances on *The Office* and *Shark Tank*, Wally has seen unparalleled success and serious failure. In 2020, Amos was still going strong at 83 years old with his latest venture, Della's Cookies, proving that the entrepreneurial spirit never fades.

To understand the story of Wally Amos, we have to start at the beginning, when the man who would become "Famous" had nothing but a hunger for success and an aunt who taught him the value in one delicious chocolate chip cookie.

The Early Days

Wally's early life was one of hardship and poverty. An only child, Amos's parents had difficulty supporting their son, who often had to walk four miles to and from school just to save on bus fare.

After his parents' divorce at age 12, he was sent to live with his Aunt Della in Harlem. In a segregated neighborhood in one of America's toughest cities, young Wally Amos found the passion that would eventually make him famous.

Aunt Della showed her nephew how to make chocolate chip cookies that people would love. The secret? "I put more chocolate in mine," Amos would tell a reporter decades later.

In 1954, Wally Amos dropped out of high school to join the United States Air Force. Amos's time in the military undoubtedly taught him discipline, and his later college education in secretarial work earned him a job at William Morris, then the largest and most successful talent agency in the world. Starting as a mail room clerk, Amos worked his way up the corporate ladder, eventually becoming the first black talent scout in American history.

His time at William Morris was full of successes. Wally became the head of the newly formed rock 'n roll division at the company, signing many best-selling artists of the 1960s. But despite his achievements, Wally remained unfulfilled in his work.

"I got tired of not making any money and constantly giving all my energy to someone else," he later admitted in a magazine interview. "I realized that I could still be in the same situation ten years from then." Amos's attitude is very common with self-starters and entrepreneurs. He wanted to be his own boss and start something he could build himself—and make a ton of money in the process.

In 1975, he did just that.

The Dough Rises

With a $25,000 loan from two of his musician friends, Amos started what would become his most notable venture: the Famous Amos cookie store on Los Angeles' Sunset Boulevard. His investors didn't have to wait long to see returns; by 1976, Amos had opened two more franchises on the West Coast and secured a distribution deal with famous New York retailer Bloomingdale's.

Amos's success came from pure hard work. He regularly put in 18-hour days and tirelessly promoted his brand. Anyone who's seen a package of Famous Amos cookies can recall Amos's trademark Panama hat and Hawaiian shirt from the company logo. In the 1980s, both articles of clothing hung proudly in the Smithsonian museum.

His company expanded nationwide, bringing gourmet cookies to a hungry nation. He was invited to march in the Macy's Thanksgiving Day Parade. In 1986, President Ronald Reagan awarded him one of the first Entrepreneurial Excellence Awards. Famous Amos cleared millions in sales and became one of the most well-known brands in the snack industry.

But by 1989, the cookie had begun to crumble.

A New Recipe For Success

The story of Famous Amos's eventual failure is a complicated one. Amos was still running the company when they began posting major losses. The company was sold to one holding corporation, then another. Frustrated by this constant change, Amos eventually reduced his role in the company before he was kicked out entirely. He lived every entrepreneur's nightmare; he'd lost control of the very enterprise he'd founded. Amos's name and likeness were still on the package when he was forced out.

Wally attempted to use his own name in his next cookie making venture. The Wally Amos Presents Chip & Cookie company opened its doors in 1991 and immediately ran into trouble with the owners of Famous Amos. They contended that he couldn't use the Amos name, which they owned the rights to.

The owners of Famous Amos sued. Wally lost the case. He had to close his newest company and take on sizable debt.

This is where some people would give up.

Not Wally Amos. Undeterred, he started the Uncle Nonamè Cookie Company and included a recipe for lemonade on every package.

Amos explained this packaging choice in an interview with *Parade* magazine. "I want to tell people that if life hands them a lemon, they can turn it into lemonade." This sense of humor and unstoppable spirit are what have kept him in the game for so many decades. However, while the Uncle Nonamé Cookie Company posted a profit early on, it eventually closed.

Amos then opened another company. He is still baking and selling cookings as of 2020.

What Wally Didn't Know

"You're a legend!" Mark Cuban declared during Wally Amos's 2016 appearance on television's *Shark Tank*. The man behind Famous Amos basked in the applause and adoration of the five business magnates as he promoted his latest company: The Cookie Kahuna. Dressed head to toe in watermelon-patterned clothing, Amos made a memorable appearance and charmed the panel with his spirit and wit.

Yet he received no investments. All five of the sharks passed on his business opportunity.

It may seem strange that such a notable figure in the snack industry couldn't get funding for his project. While failed bids are common on *Shark Tank*, most applicants don't have decades of experience in their niche. What went wrong?

Perhaps it was Amos reading his sales figures off a notecard, admitting that he's "not a numbers guy." While that poor start didn't help his sales pitch, it was the margins on the product—$5.25 to manufacture the cookies, which sold for $7.89—that really killed the deal.

Huffington Post called these numbers "some of the worst

margins ever seen [on *Shark Tank*]." One would think Wally Amos would know better, but in reality, it's not so surprising.

Amos has a passion for starting and expanding companies. He's good at making cookies and loves his work. Like many entrepreneurs, he focuses entirely on what he does well, at the expense of what's important. He will always be remembered as a master marketer!

However, while numbers and sales figures may be less fun than chocolate chips and cookie dough, they're essential to keeping a business running. It doesn't matter how delicious your product is if you neglect your bottom line.

Unfortunately, The Cookie Kahuna couldn't survive. The company folded months after the *Shark Tank* episode aired.

Life Lessons From A Cookie King

Wally Amos is upfront about his failures and the lessons he's learned from starting so many businesses. From working as a mail room clerk to a talent agent, to becoming the king of the cookie world. And losing it all, he's seen the best and worst of what entrepreneurship can look like.

Amos reminds us that being a successful entrepreneur isn't just about mastering one thing; you have to bring everything together.

He's happy to share what he's learned. Fans of Wally Amos adore his self-help books, which have humorous titles like *The Cookie Never Crumbles* and *Watermelon Magic*. He's an endless self-promoter, an expert in branding, and an unmistakable figure wherever he goes. Investors love his charm and have been willing to fund his newest projects all the way up to the present day.

It's not just books either. Amos's appearance on *The Office* in 2012 brought him renewed attention from a new legion of fans. Thrust back into the limelight, he was able to secure funding for his latest project: Aunt Della's Cookies, which he operates out of Charlotte, North Carolina.

"This is my last company, I can tell you that for sure. Put that on my tombstone: 'He died starting one last cookie company,'" he said in 2018, before bursting into laughter during an interview with *Charlotte Magazine*.

Most 83-year-olds are well into retirement. Wally Amos, however, is a *different* kind of cookie. A born entrepreneur, he clearly knows the only thing to do in life is to keep moving forward, keep trying new ideas, and keep doing what you love. You have to be willing to believe in yourself! And when you fail, pick yourself back up.

And, most importantly, make sure people love your product. For Wally Amos, the cookie king, business has never been sweeter.

Fun Facts

- Wally's side passion was supporting literacy.
- Wally always claimed that he has been in business to make friends, not to sell treats.

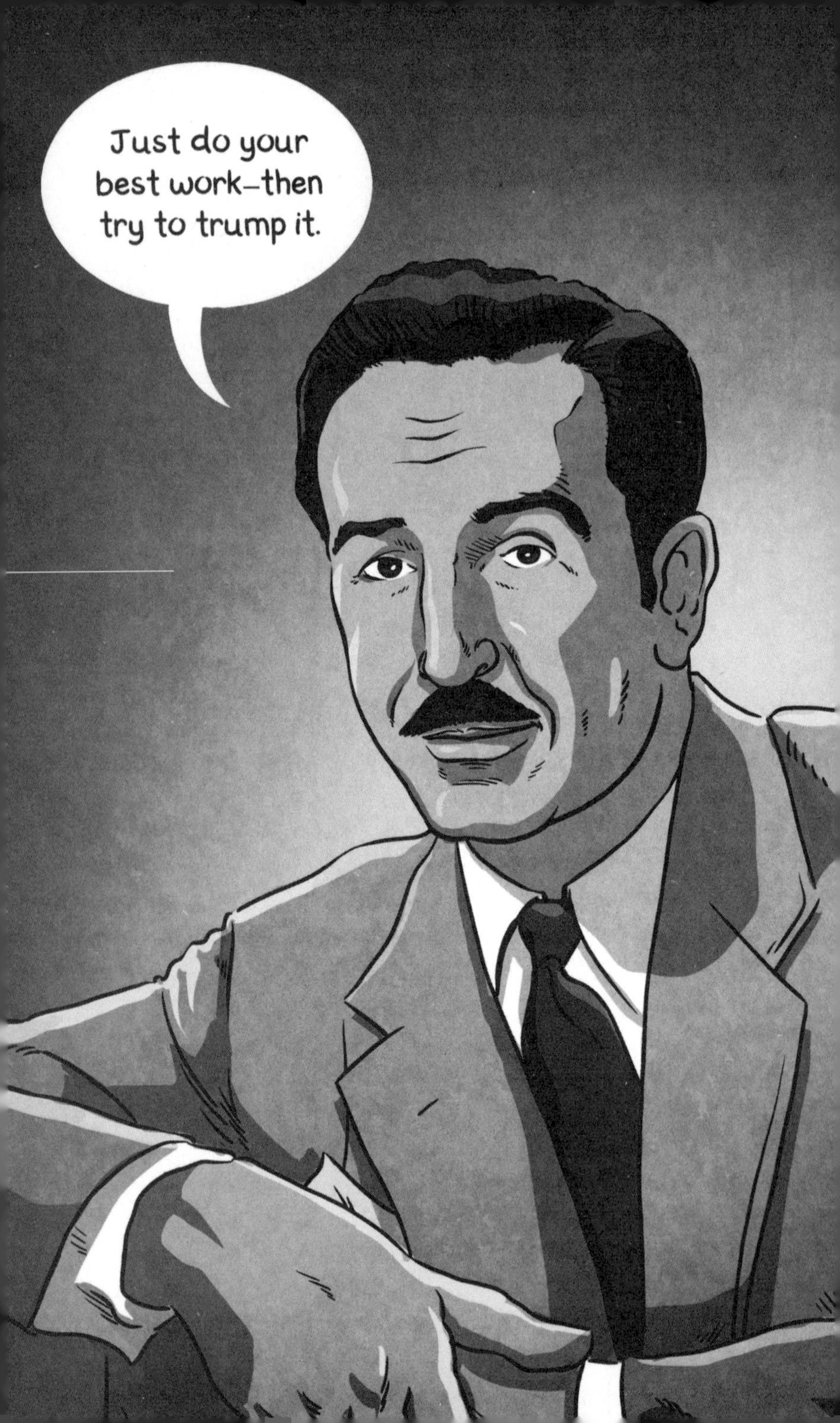
Just do your best work–then try to trump it.

Walt
DISNEY

The name Disney has become synonymous with innovation because Walt wasn't afraid of trying new things, making mistakes, and trying again. He maintained this spirit of curiosity and a thrill for improving the world during his entire life.

"I think it's important to have a good hard failure when you're young."

The Man Behind the Brand

Walt Disney is a name synonymous with theme parks, animated films, and unforgettable characters. Over 50 years after his death, his name still reigns atop a global empire. Behind that name is an artist, businessman, filmmaker, and cultural icon responsible for bringing more joy to men and women across the world than any other individual during the twentieth century. One chapter could never encompass the life and achievements of Disney. Nevertheless, one particular life lesson we can focus on is the importance of learning from failure.

In today's world, failure has become something to fear and avoid, but should it be? The value of perseverance, persistence, and learning from failure cannot be overstated. Walt Disney embodied this life principle by taking his failures and turning them into new opportunities. For example, he was fired as a commercial artist and had his first two animation businesses fail after bankruptcy. If Walt never had to overcome those major life obstacles, he might have never gone on to create the Disney conglomerate we know today. Even after those failures, he knew he was on to something big. He had a vision that he would never let go of until the day he died: find creative ways to bring the most joy and happiness to everyone around him. He wouldn't let anyone stop him from pursuing this goal.

Turbulent Upbringing

While he was growing up, Walt Disney watched his father, Elias, experience multiple failures. He was an unsuccessful businessman and farmer throughout his life. He attempted to be a fiddler in Colorado, an orange grower in Florida, a newspaper deliveryman in Kansas City, and a construction worker in Chicago. Even with his shortcomings and missteps, Elias demonstrated a resilient mindset that imprinted itself on Walt.

Elias never stopped trying to provide for his family. He never quit, and that was a powerful lesson for Disney: when faced with failure, pull yourself back up and try again.

Disney had an interesting childhood, from reluctantly helping on the farm where he grew up, to helping his father sell newspapers and candy in Kansas City, to then driving an ambulance in France during World War II at only seventeen. His mind always fell back to one thing: creating art.

The Road to California

After returning from the war in France, Disney moved to Kansas City to pursue a career in commercial artistry. Financial success never materialized while he lived here, but he used the opportunity to hone his artistic craft.

His brother Roy got him a job at the Pesmen-Rubin Art Studio. After landing this job, Disney shouted with joy to his Aunt Margaret, "Auntie, they're paying me to draw!" Merely a month later, his joy quickly fizzled when he was laid off. But it wasn't for nothing. His short tenure with the studio was worth far more than he could have thought; Disney received his first taste of being a paid artist and could never let that go. He tried opening his first commercial art business. Unfortunately, little money was brought in, which forced Disney to rejoin the traditional job market.

Although it wasn't his first choice, he didn't stray far from the world of art. Disney reluctantly took a job with the Kansas City Film Ad Company, making one-minute advertisements to appear before movies and live action films. This decision opened the door for him to learn the art of film animation, which proved to be a necessary skill for Disney to later develop his cherished films.

Disney continued to develop his skills and soon had the confidence to open a small business again: Laugh-O-Gram Films, Inc. This time around, he began to explore the use of animation with his art, experimenting with ways to grasp the attention of the audience. During his experimentation, Walt created *Alice in Cartoonland*. In it, a real little girl entered the cartoon world. It started off as a short animated film about seven minutes long, but was later developed into the renowned *Alice in Wonderland* film.

At one point during this business venture, Disney was forced to eat dog food just to save enough money to pay rent! Still young and inexperienced in the workings of a business, he entered into a costly financial deal that ultimately led to the downfall of his company. After only two years, Laugh-O-Grams, Inc. filed for bankruptcy. He could have easily quit in frustration and left his dream behind him, but instead, he decided to take the lessons learned from his early life on the road with him all the way to sunny California.

Unbreakable Bond

Disney arrived in Hollywood, California, with a mere 40 dollars to his name. He brought someone along with him to explore new and grand opportunities in Hollywood: his older brother Roy. Their relationship stayed constant throughout Disney's life. They had an unbreakable bond. Throughout their lives, Roy always maintained contact with his brother, continually keeping a watchful eye on the successes and obstacles he faced. Whenever Disney needed brotherly advice or help to pick himself back up after a failure in his career, Roy was there to mentor him through it. They were more than brothers; they were best friends. They ended up surprising the world by being a tremendous business duo as well.

Disney was a man with goals that he was driven to achieve. One of those goals was working with his brother: "I wanted Roy and me to be partners, that was all. I mean, we just wanted to be partners—I wanted it." In 1923 his wish became a reality when Walt and Roy established Disney Brothers Cartoon Studio.

The two brothers had skill sets that perfectly complemented each other's. Walt Disney was the creative mind, always looking to fulfill his vision. Roy Disney kept a clean mindset, looking at the numbers and ensuring Walt's vision stayed on track financially. "My brother Walt and I first went into business together almost a half-century ago. And he was really, in my opinion, truly a genius—creative, with great determination, singleness of purpose, and drive," Roy explained.

Walt and Roy would find quick success in Hollywood when a major New York distributor, Universal Studios, made a deal to release the Alice comedies (later known as *Alice in Wonderland*). With momentum rolling and the business becoming more successful, Disney knew he needed to explore new ideas. He wanted to develop a new character for the people! Oswald the Lucky Rabbit was born. He was a new type of character for Disney, one with personality. The character was an experiment of his to insert personality through animation. Oswald was bold and adventurous. Walt was exploring methods of making his characters connect with the audience on a personal level so they could better enjoy the experience.

Unfortunately, Walt soon faced a new business obstacle. After two years, Universal Studios started firing Disney's animators. Then in 1927, they claimed that Oswald was the sole property of the studio. Disney took this failure as another lesson: never again would he allow others to get in the way of his vision. He vowed to protect the ownership of his creations.

Walt Disney was not one to be pushed around any longer. He took his work back to Hollywood to create a new and better character, and Mickey Mouse was born. Disney tried to find a distributor; ultimately, he fell short. Studios found the idea of Mickey as a terrifying giant mouse and believed no one would find that cute. MGM studios went so far as to say the character would scare women.

A daring move was needed. Disney saw the value of an up-and-coming sound revolution in 1928 that connected sound with the action of a film. Prior to this movement, films were silent. Disney understood this was a new way to evoke emotion from the audience! One issue, the musical orchestra would have to play right along with the movement of the animated film. This would require the orchestra to play perfectly throughout the entire film. But Disney was not going to allow this obstacle to keep him down. He came up with an innovative idea to print a bouncing ball on the film for the orchestra play along with.

The simple idea of using a bouncing ball worked perfectly to keep the players synchronized throughout the entire film. *Steamboat Willy* made Mickey Mouse an instant star.

Fantasy Through Entertainment

Disney was a creative innovator, a man who identified a problem in the market and found a way to fill that void. He made a career of entertaining people in a new and unique way. Disney's first great innovation came through creating animated characters that the audience could connect with, later adding sound for further immersion into the fantasy. He recognized this as a new, revolutionary way to bring people together as an entire family to bond, while diverting the audience's attention from their demanding lives and responsibilities.

His vision for animated films and movies had continued success throughout his lifetime. Disney was nominated for 59 Academy Awards—winning 22 of them—between 1931 and 1968. Throughout his life, he continued using innovative new technology to test and experiment with new ways to immerse the audience into his animations. He pioneered ways of using specially designed cameras, adding color, utilizing television, and using methods to make the animated characters appear 3-dimensional. Disney always kept his vision of bringing happiness to others in mind.

In a way, Disney envisioned creating his own utopia throughout his life—a place for people to get away and be happy. His drawings, animation, film work, character creations, and innovations were all stepping stones to his ultimate goal to bring his animations to life. He wanted to create an environment where children and families could come together.

Disney wanted to build a theme park with that vision as the foundation. Fortunately, he came to be an entrepreneur during a period that allowed entrepreneurs to pursue their dreams. He began his visionary idea for a state-of-the-art theme park. Disneyland, a $17-million investment that opened on July 17, 1955, in Anaheim, California, was an instant success. It was a place where parents and children could explore, enjoy entertainment, and meet the Disney characters they had grown to love. Disney had brought the 2D world of animated films to the real world for kids of all ages to enjoy.

Walt Disney continued to inspire and create, and with that success came a large cushion of financial stability. Though, Disney was known for being uninterested in money. For him, it was about his vision, and his terms of success came from the audience's reaction to the entertainment he created. He constantly asked himself, "Will this make an individual happy?"

That is what made Disney obsessed with the details. Everything needed to be perfect. He defined the progress of his vision by how he made each individual feel through his creations.

By the 1950s, Disney had revolutionized the world of

family-friendly entertainment. But he had one more goal in mind to fully conquer his vision. He wanted to create a world that was a place that made the everyday unforgettable, a place where people would never want to leave. This vision grew to be the Experiment Prototype Community of Tomorrow, or EPCOT. Walt and Roy Disney immediately went to work at developing this new project in Orlando, Florida.

Disney envisioned EPCOT "like the city of tomorrow ought to be. A city that caters to the people as a service function. It will be a planned, controlled community, a showcase for American industry and research, schools, cultural, and educational opportunities."

Sadly, Disney was diagnosed with lung cancer in 1966 while his new project was under construction, and he died on December 15, 1966. After his death, Roy continued the plans to finish the theme park that opened in 1971 as Walt Disney World. Although today it's the most famous theme park in the world, it would surely not meet Disney's original expectations for EPCOT. One thing is certain: he was a visionary until his death.

Today, the Walt Disney Company is the largest operator of theme parks in the world and a $50 billion firm employing more than 175,000 people.

Walt Disney will go down in history as an industrialist with an ability to entertain. His work continues to produce countless happy memories for people all over the world today. If you're going to learn any lesson from Walt Disney, remember that even when faced with multiple failures throughout his life, he never quit. He always kept his vision in front of him. There's a vision in all of us. Whether or not it becomes reality depends on what you do to make it real.

Fun Facts

- Disney drove his daughters to school every day.

- He had an obsession with trains.

- He was a high school dropout and was considering selling vacuums before catching a break working for an animation company in New York.

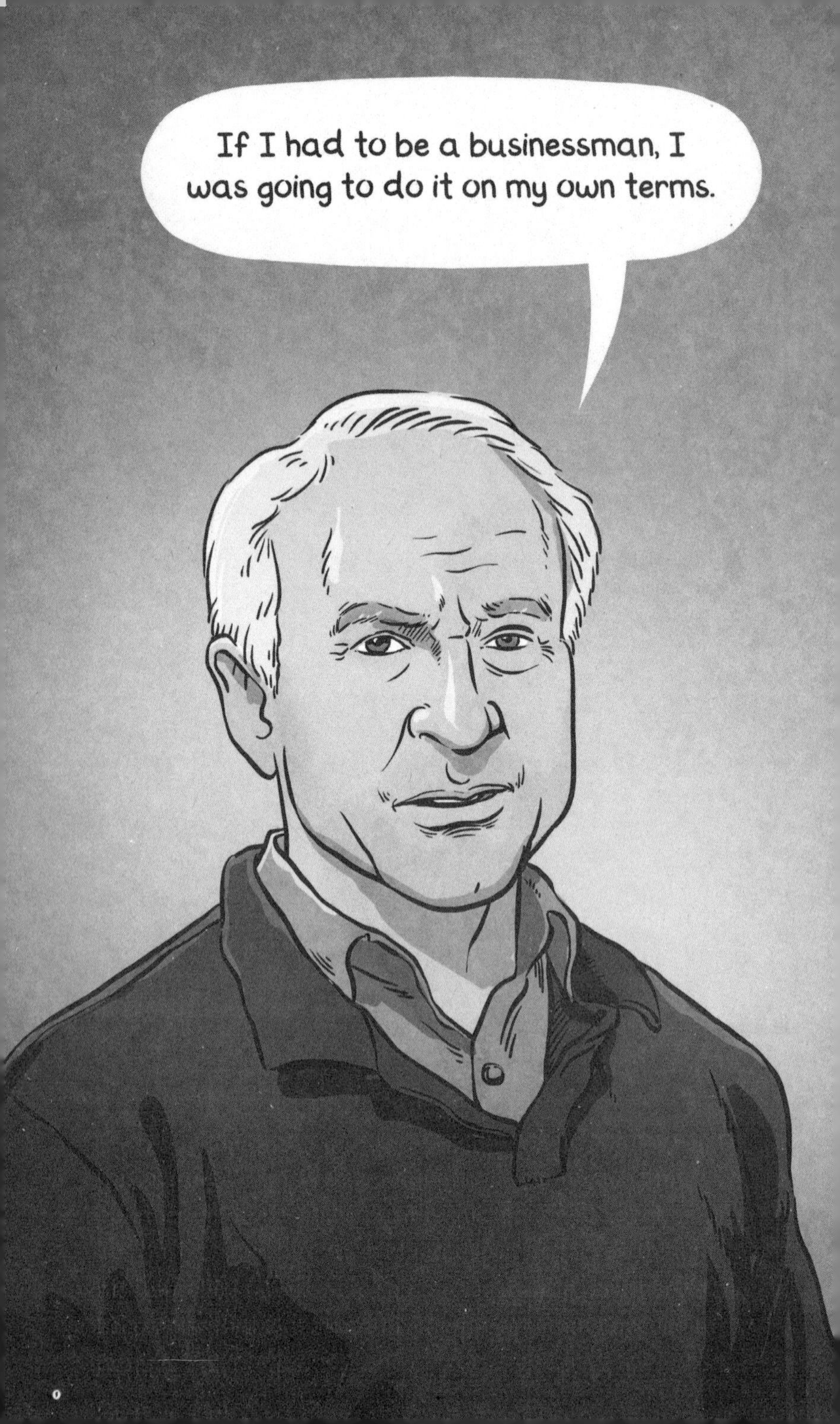
If I had to be a businessman, I was going to do it on my own terms.

Yvon
CHOUINARD

Many entrepreneurs become so lost in the work of business that they lose sight of the reason they started in the first place. Not Yvon! Through decades of innovation he never lost his passion for life and the outdoors, and made these the focus of every business decision.

"Most people hate change—it's threatening. I thrive on it."

The Patagonia Man

Do you enjoy the occasional hike? When you see the snow start to fall, do you immediately think about hitting the slopes? Do you look up a nice flat mountainside and smile as you imagine climbing it? If so, you've likely encountered one of the largest outdoor brands in the world: Patagonia.

Patagonia has become a household name. It is a clothing company that has celebrities sporting the same Patagonia fleece at red carpet events that a climber sports on a mountaintop. The mastermind behind this brand, Yvon Chouinard, started out by simply wanting to earn money to fund his own climbing habit.

Chouinard had two ambitions: to make products that enhance the outdoor experience and to make quality clothes that are durable and long lasting. By always asking how he could make everyday items better, he continued to find ways to add value to his gear. If he found value in the improvements he was making, maybe others would as well.

His humble mindset of wanting to improve upon the experiences he loved is what helped create the billion dollar company we know today.

The Climb

Yvon Chouinard developed a passion for the outdoors from a young age. He looked at the outdoors as a place to explore and find endless adventure. The outdoors represented a place to fulfill the innate desire for curiosity, to test your limits, and to find ways to overcome obstacles.

For Chouinard, rock climbing became the ultimate outdoor experience.

Chouinard started climbing in 1953 at just 14 years old as a member of the Southern California Falconry Club. His passion for rock climbing had him finding new groups to join, new peaks to conquer, and new lessons to learn. He continually tried to quench his thirst for adventure by finding bigger and bigger natural rock walls to conquer-- seeking out new challenges to overcome.

In the 1950s, rock climbing gear wasn't as innovative and easy to use as it is today. At the time, the spikes and pegs (pitons) necessary for rock climbing were not reusable like today. The old school pitons Chouinard used as a child were made of soft iron. After placing them in the rock, they were left there--one and done. This wasn't much of a problem for Chouinard early into his rock climbing adventures as popular climbing locations already had the pitons placed and ready for climbing. But Chouinard's curiosity had him looking for a new challenge.

Chouinard looked beyond the popular rock climbing locations and found himself a climbing crew with a desire for adventure. His growing passion for rock climbing had him conquering multi-day ascents in Yosemite National Park in California. However, because the pitons were single use, he had to haul around hundreds of them. This made long climbs cumbersome and costly.

Chouinard needed a solution! He had developed an entrepreneurial mindset early on, as he continually worked to improve the gear he used for his surfing, hiking, and climbing. When Chouinard learned that one of his climbing crew friends was a blacksmith, his curiosity was sparked. This was the perfect skill to help improve his gear.

In 1957, Chouinard was ready to explore his new found fascination with blacksmithing. In hopes of creating more efficient climbing gear, he went to an old junkyard to hunt for hidden treasures that could be used as materials. After wading through the endless piles of junk, he finally struck gold by finding a coal-fired forge—the perfect blacksmithing oven.

But now he needed the tools to forge, bend, and cut the smoldering hot metal from his new oven. His hunt continued. Chouinard was on the verge of giving up after searching for endless hours when he struck gold again by finding a 138-pound anvil, tongs, and hammers. He finally found the necessary tools to craft the reusable pitons he envisioned!

For Chouinard, merely asking himself the simple question of how to improve something allowed him to open his mind to imagine a solution.

As with many activities Chouinard became fixated on, he developed a knack for skillful blacksmithing. He made his first reusable climbing pitons out of old harvester blades. He and his climbing buddies were eager to try out the new creation; it was the moment of truth. Chouinard and his climbing crew took the pitons for a spin on some of his favorite climbing spots from Lost Arrow Chimney to the North Face of Sentinel Rock in Yosemite. They were a booming success.

The climbing world was a well-connected community, so word of Chouinard's creation spread fast. His friends were lining up to try his new invention. He never envisioned his creation as a business opportunity; he merely wanted to improve upon an activity that brought him joy. But as his friends, and friends of friends, started lining up to test out his new pitons, an entrepreneur was born.

When Chouinard encountered an issue with his gear, he would then consider whether other people were experiencing this problem. Luckily, he was always surrounded by his climbing buddies who were happy to provide feedback.

Pursuing a Dream

Chouinard was able to make two pitons per hour. He sold them for $1.50 each ($14, adjusted for inflation). His first shop was not glamorous. He had set up shop in his parents' backyard in Burbank, California. Luckily, most of his blacksmithing tools were portable, so Chouinard packed up all his necessary tools and drove along the coast of California—surfing by day and blacksmithing at night.

Chouinard understood the importance of his innovation but never allowed himself to forget his love of the outdoors—be it surfing, hiking, fishing, or climbing (whatever was in season!). This is what drove him to create the pitons, not only to fund his activities, but improve the enjoyment others had in the sport. He found joy in helping other people explore their curiosity.

For a few years, he would craft his pitons during the winter months, spend fall and summer in Yosemite climbing, and the summer surfing and traveling to Wyoming for even more climbing. Along the way, he would sell his new piton.

Was he living the dream? Not exactly. At one point during this period, he was living off of canned cat tuna, oatmeal, potatoes, and poached squirrel—just enough to get him by. His business venture wasn't lucrative at first, even though his improved pitons were so popular that he wasn't able to keep up with the demand for them. Something needed to change.

Chouinard upgraded his tools and joined forces with Tom Frost, an aeronautical engineer and fellow climber, in 1965. Tom helped improve the design and look of the gear. They worked to redesign and enhance every climbing tool, making them stronger, lighter, simpler, and more durable, all while ramping up production to meet the rising demand. By 1970, Chouinard Equipment was the largest supplier of climbing equipment in the United States.

Following customer demand, Chouinard got out of the piton business. It turned out that their innovative pitons were actually having adverse effects on the rocks. Pounding in and then removing the spikes was slowly chipping away at the rocks. With constant climber traffic, the popular locations were becoming disfigured. Some areas even became dangerous as rocks in certain areas became more fragile after enduring repeated chipping.

Chouinard found himself faced with another problem to overcome, not only for his company but for the rock climbing locations he loved to conquer.

To meet this rising concern, Chouinard developed aluminum chocks that could be wedged by hand. This avoided the hammering and forceful removal of the spikes.

When faced with a problem he went right back to the drawing board. The result? The product was more efficient, cheaper to create, and environmentally friendly. He tried to make it a point to stick with his principles and improve upon the outdoor experience while always remembering to respect the outdoors he loved.

Patagonia

Before the current trend of outdoor wear as everyday fashion, sportswear was gray. Through the 1960s, men may have a couple of pairs of sweatpants, a t-shirt, and sweatshirt that would cover most of their activewear needs. This attire was often cheap. Most just went to a secondhand store to buy some old clothes to wear. Typical mountain attire was an old button up shirt, old chinos or a cut-off pair of chinos. However, sweatshirts and pants and secondhand clothes were not durable and could not hold up to the rigors of the wild.

Even the real mountaineers like Chouinard couldn't find a go-to American clothing line to meet their needs.

Chouinard found himself faced with another obstacle to overcome: he needed something to withstand the changing weather conditions and the various obstacles of mountain climbing, fishing, and hiking. He recognized a solution by chance.

While on a climbing trip in Scotland, Chouinard was visiting a local clothing store when a rugby shirt caught his eye. He noticed the more durable material, the higher quality knitting, the collar that could protect against climbing slings, and, as a bonus, the shirt had color! It was a perfect shirt to replace his old climbing t-shirts.

Back in the United States, Chouinard's climbing buddies soon started asking where he got the shirt. They, too, noticed the better material, durability, and colors. They were champing at the bit to get their hands on one! Chouinard's entrepreneurial mind was always churning. He ordered the durable clothing from overseas and started selling it to all those who were interested.

Chouinard kicked off a new athletic-wear fashion craze, and Patagonia was born!

Staying True to Himself

Chouinard is a reluctant businessman, possibly from a misconceived image of them; he views politicians and businessmen as "the source of all evil." However, he has made it a point to stay true to what he believes is right, which has kept him humble. His thought process has remained the same: Does it make my outdoor experience better? Does it make others' experiences better? Does it make the environment better? Am I still having fun, and are my employees having fun?

Chouinard tries to answer an emphatic yes to all of those questions. If he finds himself answering no, he contemplates whether what he is doing is truly what drives his passion.

He translates these principles into a unique managing style. Often creators want to be hands-on when growing their product by having everything run through them.

Chouinard thinks differently; he wants to find people who have a similar work ethic as himself. He wants people who are self-motivated. He didn't enjoy telling people what to do, so he made it a point to find people who were good workers and could just be left alone.

He made it clear that he expected that the people who work for him still find time to surf, fish, mountain climb, play volleyball at the office, or go skiing, because he wanted his employees to be driven by the same passion he found himself driven by: the outdoors. This resulted in building his business with the same community focus that helped him begin. It was a place for feedback from people who shared the same passions. The result is a company that prioritizes personal responsibility, focus on family, and environmental consciousness.

With the successful growth of his company, he was able to gather funds for various environmental groups he found important. Since 1985, 1% of all Patagonia sales have been set aside to finance environmental groups across the world. He didn't need the government to tell him the right thing to do, and with the success of his company, he's been able to do more to protect the environment than the government likely ever will.

Takeaway

One thing about Chouinard is undeniable: he has an entrepreneurial mindset. He looks at a product and thinks, "How can I make this better?" As Chouinard and Patagonia continue to grow today, he makes it a priority to maintain his vision: improve upon products, respect the environment, and enjoy the outdoors.

Fun Facts

- Since 1984, Chouinard's business has maintained an open office plan. Chouinard doesn't even have his own office.

- Since the 1990s, Patagonia has placed child care facilities at their headquarters.

- The company has also made clothing repair a major part of their brand.

Ready to take the plunge?

Our hope is that after reading these stories and finding inspiration in the lives of many past and present entrepreneurs, you'll be ready to follow in their footsteps and find—or create—an opportunity to serve others through the free market.

We've had some experience with entrepreneurship ourselves… lemonade stands, a family theater, and more. It's hard work, but super rewarding! You can learn a lot along the way—especially when you fail.

See, no one is perfect at this stuff. Our mistakes can teach us some of the greatest lessons, and it often takes several tries before you've identified the right opportunity and have the skills enough to succeed.

But the journey is worth it—and while there is dignity and importance in all kinds of jobs, there's something special about forging your own path and growing as a person through entrepreneurship.

Consider giving it a try—but buckle up, because the journey can be bumpy at times!

—The Tuttle Twins

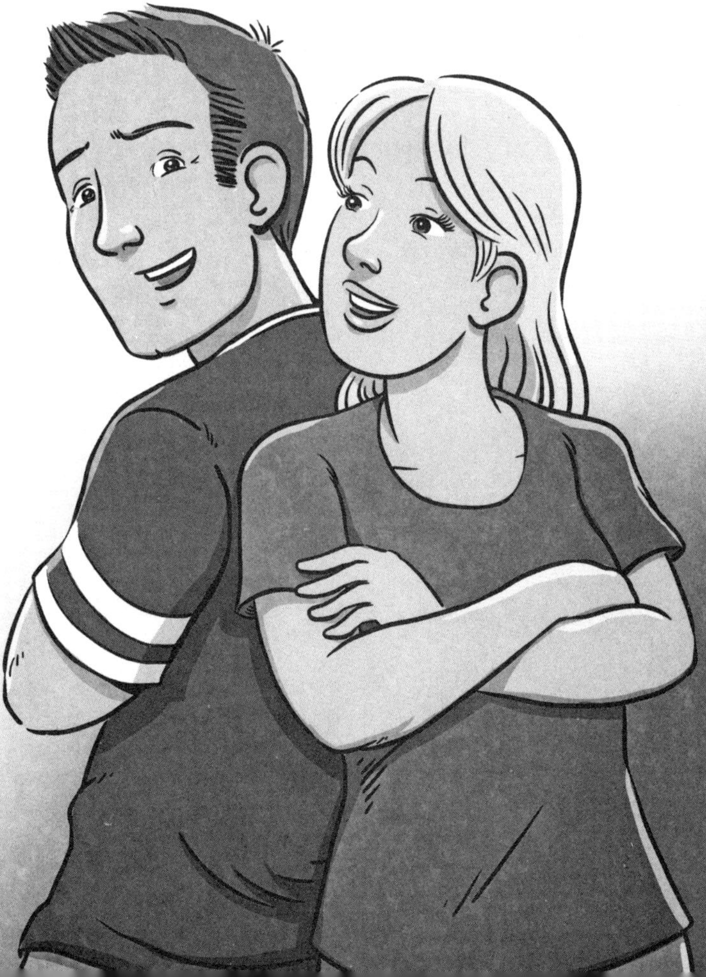